Books by Viktor E. Frankl

Man's Search for Meaning
Psychotherapy and Existentialism
The Unconscious God
The Unheard Cry for Meaning

Published by WASHINGTON SQUARE PRESS

VIKTOR E. FRANKL

THE UNHEARD CRY FOR MEANING

Psychotherapy and Humanism

WASHINGTON SQUARE PRESS

PUBLISHED BY POCKET BOOKS NEW YORK

A Washington Square Press Publication of
POCKET BOOKS, a division of Simon & Schuster, Inc.
1230 Avenue of the Americas, New York, N.Y. 10020

Published by arrangement with Simon and Schuster
Library of Congress Catalog Card Number: 77-25848

ISBN: 0-671-54163-3

First Washington Square Press printing February, 1985

10 9 8 7 6 5 4 3 2 1

WASHINGTON SQUARE PRESS, WSP and colophon are
registered trademarks of Simon & Schuster, Inc.

Printed in the U.S.A.

To Harry or Marion
an unborn child

A special word of gratitude to my wife, Eleonore Katharina, whom I thank for all the sacrifices she has made throughout the years for the sake of helping me to help others. Indeed, she merits the words that Professor Jacob Needleman once inscribed in a book of his that he dedicated to her on one of my lecture tours, which I made, as I always do, in her company. "To the warmth," he wrote, "that accompanies the light."

May the warmth long persist when the light has dimmed away.

Viktor E. Frankl

Contents

Preface

THIS BOOK CONTINUES THE SEQUENCE THAT WAS initiated by two of its predecessors, *Psychotherapy and Existentialism* and *The Unconscious God: Psychotherapy and Theology.*

It was originally planned as a compilation of selected essays, but as I revised and expanded the contents it became ever more clear that, although the papers that had now been made into chapters were wholes, they still were interconnected by a thread. Even more important, the first two chapters discussed the three main tenets on which the system of logotherapy is based: the will to meaning, the meaning of life, the freedom of will.

Logotherapy is usually subsumed under the categories of existential psychiatry or humanistic psychology. However, the reader of my books may have noticed that I have made some critical remarks regarding existentialism, or at least regarding what is *called* existentialism. Similarly, he will find in this book some attacks directed at *so-called* humanism, or as I call it myself, pseudo-humanism. He should not be surprised: I am against pseudo-logotherapy as well.

Let us briefly review the history of psychotherapy in order to determine the place of both existentialism and humanism in psychiatry and psychology. All of us have learned the lesson of the greatest spirit in psychotherapy, Sigmund Freud. I, too! (I wonder if the reader is aware of the fact that as early as 1924 a paper of mine was published in the *International Journal of Psychoanalysis,* upon the personal invitation and intercession of Sigmund Freud.) He has taught us *to unmask the neurotic,* to reveal the hidden, unconscious motivations underlying his behavior. However, as I never tire of saying, unmasking has to stop at the point where the psychoanalyst is confronted with what can no longer be unmasked, simply because it is authentic. But if some "unmasking psychologists" (that is what psychoanalysts once called themselves!) do not stop when confronted with something authentic, they still are unmasking something. This is their own hidden motivation, their unconscious desire to devalue, debase and depreciate what is genuine, what is genuinely human, in man.

In the meantime, behavior therapy based on learning theory has gained much of the ground on which psychoanalysis stood for so long in an unquestioned position. Behavior therapists could offer evidence that many of the Freudians' etiological beliefs were merely beliefs. Neither is each and every case of neurosis traceable to early childhood traumatic experiences or to conflicts between id, ego and superego, nor did symptom substitution follow those cures which were brought about, not by psychoanalysis, but rather by short-term behavior modification (if not by spontaneous remission). Thus one may credit behaviorism with the *demythologization of neurosis*.*

Yet there remained a sense of discontent. It is not possible to cope with the ills and ailments of an age such as ours, one of meaninglessness, depersonalization and dehumanization, unless the human dimension, the dimension of human phenomena, is included in the concept of man that indispensably underlies every sort of psychotherapy, be it on the conscious or unconscious level.

Bjarne Kvilhaug, a Norwegian psychologist, contends that logotherapy has rehumanized learning theory. The late Nikolaus Petrilowitsch, of the Department of Psychiatry at the University of Mainz, West Germany, has stated that logotherapy has rehumanized psychoanalysis, and more specifically, that logotherapy—in contrast to all other schools of psychotherapy—does not remain in the dimension of neurosis. What does he mean? Psychoanalysis sees neurosis as the result of certain psychodynamics and accordingly tries to counteract it by bringing into play other psychodynamics, helpful ones such as a sound transference relationship. As to behavior therapy, it attributes neurosis to certain learning, or conditioning, processes and accordingly prescribes relearning, or reconditioning, to counteract it. In both cases, however, as Petrilowitsch so aptly noted, the therapy remains on the plane of neurosis. But logotherapy, as

---

* This formulation is not too farfetched when one considers the fact that Sigmund Freud himself described his instinct theory as a "mythology" and referred to the instincts as "mythical" entities.

he sees it, goes beyond this plane, following man into the human dimension, where it may draw upon the resources that are available there alone—resources such as the uniquely human capacities of self-transcendence and self-detachment.

The latter capacity is mobilized whenever the logotherapeutic technique of paradoxical intention is practiced; the former is equally important in diagnosis and therapy. Without envisaging self-transcendence, or for that matter, one of its aspects, the will to meaning, we can never diagnose a noögenic neurosis which derives from the frustration of the will to meaning; nor can we appeal to it or, if it has been replaced, evoke it out of the patient's unconscious. That this may sometimes constitute our principal assignment has been shown on strictly empirical grounds: it has been evidenced by statistical research that the will to meaning has an obvious "survival value."

Something parallel has been proven, also on strictly empirical grounds, with respect to self-detachment: namely, that it is an important "coping mechanism," built in, as it were, in the human psyche. As I shall show, this holds in particular for that aspect of self-detachment which is represented by humor.

Summing up, one may say that psychoanalysis has taught us *to unmask the neurotic,* and behaviorism has taught us *to demythologize neurosis.* Now, as Petrilowitsch and Kvilhaug see it, logotherapy is teaching us *to "rehumanize" both psychoanalysis and behaviorism.* But this would be an oversimplification, for there is not only a sequence but also a confluence. Today one may come across such statements as that made by the outstanding West German Freudian

Wolfgang Loch, that "in essence the psychoanalytic dialogue is an endeavour to create a new meaning of life."* The director of the Behavior Therapy Center in New York, Leonard Bachelis, also has been quoted to the effect that many undergoing therapy at the center have good jobs and are successful but want to kill themselves because they find life meaningless.†

So, there is convergence in sequence. As to *logotherapy*, however, I for one have been teaching that it *is not a panacea* and therefore is open to cooperation with other psychotherapeutic approaches and open to its own evolution. It is true that both psychodynamically and behavioristically oriented schools largely ignore the humanness of human phenomena. They are still sold on reductionism, as this still dominates the scene of psychotherapeutic training, and reductionism is the very opposite of humanism. Reductionism is subhumanism, I would say. Confining itself to subhuman dimensions, biased by a narrow concept of scientific truth, it forces phenomena into a Procrustean bed, a preconceived pattern of interpretation, whether this be along the lines of dynamic analysis or of learning theory.

And yet each of these schools has made a valuable contribution. Logotherapy in no way invalidates the sound and sober findings of such great pioneers as Freud, Adler, Pavlov, Watson or Skinner. Within their respective dimensions, each of these schools has its say. But their real significance and value become visible only if we place them within a higher, more

---

* *Psyche*, XXX, 10, 1976, pp. 865–98.
† *American Psychological Association Monitor*, May 1976.

inclusive dimension, within the human dimension. Here, to be sure, man can no longer be seen as a being whose basic concern is to satisfy drives and gratify instincts or, for that matter, to reconcile id, ego and superego; nor can the human reality be understood merely as the outcome of conditioning processes or conditioned reflexes. Here man is revealed as a being in search of meaning—a search whose futility seems to account for many of the ills of our age. How then can a psychotherapist who refuses *a priori* to listen to the "unheard cry for meaning" come to grips with the mass neurosis of today?

There are many things in my papers and books, including this book, that I am sure will seem, at least on first sight, outdated. But I am equally sure that some of them are timely. Just consider the worldwide emergence and persistence of the feeling of meaninglessness. If this is the mass neurosis of the seventies, I may say in all humility that I predicted its increase and spread in the fifties, and prior to that, provided a therapy in the thirties.

VIKTOR E. FRANKL

Vienna, on the first day of spring, 1977

THE UNHEARD CRY
FOR MEANING

The Unheard Cry
for Meaning*

A LITERAL TRANSLATION OF THE TERM "LO-
gotherapy" is "therapy through meaning." Of course,
it could also be translated as "healing through meaning," although this would bring in a religious overtone
that is not necessarily present in logotherapy. In any
case, logotherapy is a meaning-centered (psycho-)
therapy.

The notion of a *therapy through meaning* is the very
reverse of the traditional conceptualization of psychotherapy, which could rather be formulated as *meaning
through therapy*. Indeed, if traditional psychotherapy
squarely faces the issue of meaning and purpose at
all—that is, if it takes meaning and purpose at face
value rather than reducing them to mere fake values,
as by deducing them from "defense mechanisms" or
"reaction formations"†—it does so in the vein of a

---

* Based on a lecture titled "Therapy Through Meaning," delivered
at the University of California at Berkeley, February 13, 1977.

† To repeat an improvisation I made in the question-and-answer
period following a lecture of mine, I said that, as to myself, I am not
prepared to live for the sake of my reaction formations, nor to die
for the sake of my defense mechanisms.

recommendation that you just have your Oedipal situation settled, just get rid of your castration fears, and you will be happy, you will actualize your self and your own potentialities, and you will become what you were meant to be. In other words, meaning will come to you by itself. Doesn't it sound somewhat like, Seek ye first the kingdom of Freud and Skinner, and all these things will be added unto you?

But it did not work out that way. Rather, it turned out that, *if* a neurosis could be removed, more often than not *when* it was removed a vacuum was left. The patient was beautifully adjusted and functioning, but meaning was missing. The patient had not been taken as a human being, that is to say, a being in steady search of meaning; and this search for meaning, which is so distinctive of man, had not been taken seriously at its face value, but was seen as a mere rationalization of underlying unconscious psychodynamics. It had been overlooked or forgotten that if a person has found the meaning sought for, he is prepared to suffer, to offer sacrifices, even, if need be, to give his life for the sake of it. Contrariwise, if there is no meaning he is inclined to take his life, and he is prepared to do so even if all his needs, to all appearances, have been satisfied.

All this was brought home to me by the following report, which I received from a former student of mine: At an American university, 60 students who had attempted suicide were screened afterward, and 85 percent said the reason had been that "life seemed meaningless." Most important, however, 93 percent of these students suffering from the apparent meaninglessness of life "were actively engaged socially, were performing well academically, and were on good terms with their family groups." What we have here, I would say, is an unheard cry for meaning, and it certainly is not limited to only one university. Consider the staggering suicide rates among American college students, second only to traffic accidents as the most frequent cause of death. Suicide *attempts* might be fifteen times more frequent.

This happens in the midst of affluent societies and in the midst of welfare states! For too long we have been dreaming a dream from which we are now waking up: the dream that if we just improve the socioeconomic situation of people, everything will be okay, people will become happy. The truth is that as the *struggle for survival* has subsided, the question has emerged: *survival for what?* Ever more people today have the means to live, but no meaning to live for.*

On the other hand, we see people being happy under adverse, even dire, conditions. Let me quote from a letter I received from Cleve W., who wrote it when he was Number 049246 in an American state prison: "Here in prison . . . there are more and more blissful opportunities to serve and grow. I'm really happier now than I've ever been." Notice: happier than ever— in prison!

---

* There is a parallel to this state of affairs on the ontogenetic, rather than the phylogenetic, level. As a former teaching assistant of mine at Harvard University could show, among graduates of that university who went on to lead quite successful, ostensibly happy lives, a huge percentage complained of a deep sense of futility, asking themselves what all their success had been for. Does this not suggest that what today is so often referred to as "midlife crisis" is basically a crisis of meaning?

Or let me take up a letter that I recently received from a Danish family doctor: "For half a year my very dear father was seriously ill with cancer. The last three months of his life he lived in my house—looked after by my beloved wife and myself. What I really want to tell you is that those three months were the most blessed time in the lives of my wife and me. Being a doctor and a nurse, of course, we had the resources to cope with everything, but I shall never in my life forget all the evenings when I read him sentences from your book. He knew for three months that his illness was fatal . . . but he never gave a complaint. Until his last evening I kept telling him how happy we were that we could experience this close contact for those last weeks, and how poor we would have been if he had just died from a heart attack lasting a few seconds. Now I have not only read about these things, I have experienced them, so I can only hope that I shall be able to meet fate the same way my father did." Again, someone is happy in the face of tragedy and in spite of suffering—but in view of meaning! Truly, there is a healing force in meaning.

Returning to the subject of therapy through meaning, does this imply that neurosis is caused in each and every case by a lack of meaning? No; the only thing I wanted to convey is the fact that *if* there is a lack of meaning, filling up the vacuum will result in a therapeutic effect, even if the neurosis was *not* caused by the vacuum! In this sense the great physician Paracelsus was right when he said that diseases originate in the realm of nature, but healing comes from the realm of the spirit. To put it in more technical terms, in the terminology of logotherapy, a neurosis is not necessarily noögenic, i.e., resulting from a sense of meaninglessness. There is still a place for psychodynamics as well as conditioning and learning processes underlying a psychogenic neurosis, which is a neurosis in the traditional sense. But logotherapy insists that beyond these pathogenic factors there is also a dimension of specifically human phenomena, such as man's search for meaning, and unless we recognize that the frustration of this search may also cause neurosis we cannot understand, let alone overcome, the ills of our age.

In this context I would like to stress that the human dimension—or, as it is also called in logotherapy, the noölogical dimension—goes beyond the psychological dimension, and thus is the higher; but being "higher" means only that it is the more inclusive, encompassing the lower dimension. Findings within the individual dimensions cannot be mutually exclusive. The uniqueness of man, his humanness, does not contradict the fact that in the psychological and biological dimensions he still is an animal.

Therefore it is perfectly legitimate for us to use the sound findings of both psychodynamically and behavioristically oriented research, and to adopt some of the techniques that are based on them. When these techniques are incorporated into a psychotherapy that follows man into the human dimension, as logotherapy does, their therapeutic effectiveness can only be enhanced.

I have spoken of the biological dimension. In fact, along with noölogical and psychological factors, somatic ones also are involved in the etiology of mental illness. At least in the etiology of psychoses (rather than neuroses) biochemistry and heredity are of some importance, even though the bulk of symptomatology is psychogenic.

Last but not least, we must note the fact that there are also sociogenic neuroses. This designation is particularly applicable to the mass neurosis of today, namely, the feeling of meaninglessness. Patients no longer complain of inferiority feelings or sexual frustration as they did in the age of Adler and Freud. Today they come to see us psychiatrists because of feelings of futility. The problem that brings them crowding into our clinics and offices now is existential frustration, their "existential vacuum"—a term I coined as long ago as 1955. I described the condition itself in publications that date back to 1946. Thus we logotherapists may say that we were aware of what was in store for the masses long before it became a widespread, worldwide phenomenon.

Albert Camus once contended "There is but one truly serious problem, and that is . . . judging whether life is or is not worth living. . . ."* I was reminded of this recently when I was given a report in which I see a confirmation of what I said before, namely, that the existential question of a meaning to life and the existential quest for a meaning to life are haunting people today more than their sexual problems. A high-school teacher invited his students to present him with any questions they might wish, and they were allowed to do so anonymously. The questions ranged from drug addiction and sex down to life on other planets, but the most frequent subject—one wouldn't believe it!—was suicide.

---

* A. Camus, *The Myth of Sisyphus*. New York, Vintage Books, 1955, p. 3.

But why should society be blamed for this state of affairs? Are we really justified in diagnosing a sociogenic neurosis? Consider today's society: it gratifies and satisfies virtually every need—except for one, the need for meaning! One may say that some needs are even created by today's society; yet the need for meaning remains unfulfilled—in the midst of and in spite of all our affluence.

The affluence of our society is reflected not only in material goods but also in leisure time. In this connection we should give a hearing to Jerry Mandel, who writes: "Technology has deprived us of the need to use our survival skills. Thus, we have developed a system of welfare which guarantees that one can survive without making any effort on one's own behalf. When as few as 15 percent of the country's labor force could in fact supply the needs of the entire population through the use of technology, then we have to face two problems: which 15 percent will work, and how will the others deal with the fact that they are dispensable, and the consequent loss of meaning? Perhaps logotherapy may have more to say to twenty-first century America than it has already said to twentieth-century America."*

Today, to be sure, we also have to cope with unintentional leisure in the form of unemployment. Unemployment may cause a specific neurosis—"unemployment neurosis," as I called it when I first described it in 1933. But again, upon closer investigation it turned out that the real cause was the confusion of one's being unemployed with his being useless and, hence,

_____
* Unpublished paper.

his life's being meaningless. Financial compensation, or for that matter social security, is not enough. Man does not live by welfare alone.

Take the typical welfare state of Austria, which is blessed with social security and is not plagued by unemployment. And yet in an interview our Chancellor Bruno Kreisky expressed his concern about the psychological conditions of the citizens, saying that what is most important and urgent today is to counteract the feeling that life is meaningless.

The feeling of meaninglessness, the existential vacuum, is increasing and spreading to the extent that, in truth, it may be called a mass neurosis. There is ample evidence in the form of publications in professional journals to indicate that it is not confined to capitalist states but can also be observed in Communist countries. It makes itself noticeable even in the Third World.*

This brings up the question of its etiology and symptoms. As to the former, let me offer you this brief explanation: Unlike other animals, man is not told by drives and instincts what he must do, and unlike man in former times, he is no longer told by traditions and traditional values what he should do. Now, lacking these directives, he sometimes does not know what he wants to do. The result? Either he does what other

---

* See Louis L. Klitzke, "Students in Emerging Africa: Humanistic Psychology and Logotherapy in Tanzania," *American Journal of Humanistic Psychology,* 9, 1969, pp. 105–26; and Joseph L. Philbrick, "A Cross-Cultural Study of Frankl's Theory of Meaning-in-Life," paper presented to a meeting of the American Psychological Association.

people do—which is conformism—or he does what other people want him to do—which is totalitarianism.

James C. Crumbaugh, Leonard T. Maholick, Elisabeth S. Lukas and Bernard Dansart have developed various logotherapeutic tests (PIL, SONG and Logo tests) to ascertain the degree of existential frustration in a given population, and thus it is also possible empirically to verify and validate my hypothesis on the origin of the existential vacuum. With reference to the role ascribed to the decay of traditions, I see some corroboration in Diana D. Young's dissertation at the University of California. As she could evidence by tests and statistical research, young people are suffering from the existential vacuum more than older generations. Since it is also the young in whom the wane of traditions is most pronounced, this finding suggests that the crumbling of traditions is a major factor accounting for the existential vacuum. It is also in accordance with a statement made by Karol Marshal of the East Side Mental Health Center in Bellevue, Washington, who "characterized the feeling among those in the pre-30 age group who come in for help as a sense of purposelessness."*

Speaking of the young generation brings to mind a lecture I was invited to give at a major American university, and its student sponsors' insistence that the lecture be titled "Is the New Generation Mad?" It is time, indeed, to ask whether people suffering from the feeling of meaninglessness are in fact neurotic, and if so, in which sense. In short, the question reads: Is

---

* *American Psychological Association Monitor,* May 1976.

what we have called the mass neurosis of today really a neurosis?

Let me postpone answering and first briefly review the symptomatology of the existential vacuum, what I would like to call the mass neurotic triad, comprising depression, aggression and addiction.

Depression and its sequel, suicide, we have discussed. As to aggression, I refer the reader to the chapters on sports and on humanistic psychology. So we have here to elaborate only on the third aspect of the triad, in order to show that, alongside depression and aggression, addiction too is at least partially to be traced back to the feeling of meaninglessness.

Since I advanced this hypothesis numerous authors have supported it. Betty Lou Padelford devoted a dissertation to "The Influence of Ethnic Background, Sex, and Father Image upon the Relationship Between Drug Involvement and Purpose in Life" (United States International University, San Diego, January 1973). The data generated by her study of 416 students *"failed* to identify significant differences between the extent of drug involvement reported by students having a weak father image as opposed to students having a strong father image." However, a significant relationship between drug involvement and purpose in life was found beyond reasonable doubt ($r = -.23$; $p < .001$). The mean drug-involvement index for students with low purpose in life (8.90) was found to differ significantly from the mean drug-involvement index for students with high purpose in life (4.25).

Dr. Padelford also reviews the literature in the field which, like her own research, is favorable to my existential vacuum hypothesis. Nowlis addressed the question of why students were attracted to drugs and found that one reason often given was "the desire to find meaning in life." A survey of 455 students in the San Diego area, conducted by Judd *et al.* for the National Commission on Marijuana and Drug Abuse, found that users of both marijuana and hallucinogens indicated they were bothered by and had suffered over the lack of meaning of life more than had nonusers. Another study, conducted by Mirin *et al.* found that heavy drug use was correlated with a search for meaningful experience and diminished goal-directed activity. Linn surveyed 700 undergraduates at the University of Wisconsin, Milwaukee, in 1968 and reported that marijuana users, compared with nonusers, were more concerned about the meaning of life. Krippner *et al.* theorize that drug use may be a form of self-administered psychotherapy for people with existential problems, citing a 100-percent-positive response to "Have things seemed meaningless to you?" Shean and Fechtmann found that students who had smoked marijuana regularly over a six-month period scored significantly lower ($p < .001$) on Crumbaugh's Purpose-in-Life (PIL) Test than did the nonusers.

Parallel findings have been published with regard to the addiction to alcohol. Annemarie von Forstmeyer has shown in a dissertation that 18 out of 20 alcoholics looked upon their existence as meaningless and without purpose (United States International University, 1970). Accordingly, logotherapeutically oriented techniques have proved superior to other forms of therapy. When James C. Crumbaugh measured existential vacuum to compare the outcome of group logotherapy with results achieved by an alcoholic treatment unit and a marathon therapy program, "only logotherapy showed a statistically significant improvement."*

That logotherapy equally lends itself to the treatment of drug addiction has been shown by Alvin R. Fraiser at the Narcotic Addict Rehabilitation Center at Norco, California. Since 1966 he has used logotherapy in working with narcotic addicts and as a result, he says, "I have become the only counselor in the history of the institution to have three consecutive years of the highest success rate (success meaning that the addict is not returned to the institution within one year after release). My approach to dealing with the addict has resulted in a three-year 40 percent success rate as compared to an institutional average of about 11 percent (using the established approach)."

It goes without saying that, in addition to the three covert symptoms of the existential vacuum subsumed in the mass neurotic triad, also other symptoms occur, be it on a covert or an overt level. To come back to the question of whether or not the feeling of meaninglessness itself constitutes mental illness, Sigmund Freud, it is true, once wrote in a letter to Princess Bonaparte: "The moment one inquires about the sense or value of life, one is sick." But I think that, rather than exhibiting mental illness, someone worrying about the meaning of life is proving his humanness. One need not be a neurotic to be concerned with the quest for a meaning to life, but one does need to be a truly human being. After all, as I have pointed out, the search for meaning is a distinctive characteristic of being human. No other

---

* "Changes in Frankl's Existential Vacuum as a Measure of Therapeutic Outcome," *Newsletter for Research in Psychology*, 14, 1972, pp. 35–37.

animal has ever cared whether or not there is a meaning to life, not even Konrad Lorenz' grey geese. But man does.

THE WILL TO MEANING

Man is always reaching out for meaning, always setting out on his search for meaning; in other words, what I call the "will to meaning"* is even to be regarded as "man's primary concern," to quote from Abraham Maslow's comments on a paper of mine.†

It is precisely this will to meaning that remains unfulfilled by today's society—and disregarded by today's psychology. Current motivation theories see man as a being who is either *reacting* to stimuli or *abreacting* his impulses. They do not consider that actually, rather than reacting or abreacting, man is *responding*—responding to questions that life is asking him, and in that way fulfilling the meanings that life is offering.

One might argue that this is faith, not fact. Indeed, since I coined, in 1938, the term "height psychology" in order to supplement (rather than supplant) what is called "depth psychology" (that is, psychodynamically oriented psychology) I have again and again been accused of overestimating man, putting him on too high a pedestal. Let me here repeat an illustration that

---

* Viktor E. Frankl, *Der unbedingte Mensch: Metaklinische Vorlesungen*, Vienna, Franz Deuticke, 1949.
† In Anthony J. Sutich and Miles A. Vich, eds., *Readings in Humanistic Psychology*, New York, The Free Press, 1969.

has often shown to be didactically helpful. In aviation there is a business called "crabbing." Say there is a crosswind from the north and the airport where I wish to land lies due east. If I fly east I will miss my destination because my plane will have drifted to the southeast. In order to reach my destination I must compensate for this drift by crabbing, in this case by heading my plane in a direction to the north of where I want to land. It is similar with man: he too ends at a point lower than he might have unless he is seen on a higher level that includes his higher aspirations.

If we are to bring out the human potential at its best, we must first believe in its existence and presence. Otherwise man will "drift," he will deteriorate, for there is a human potential at its worst as well. We must not let our belief in the potential humanness of man blind us to the fact that *humane* humans are and probably always will be a minority. Yet it is this very fact that challenges each of us to join the minority: things are bad, but unless we do our best to improve them, everything will become worse.

Thus, rather than dismissing the concept of a will to meaning as wishful thinking, one could more justifiably conceive of it as a self-fulfilling prophecy. There is something to Anatole Broyard's comment, "If 'shrink' is the slang term for the Freudian analyst, then the logotherapist ought to be called 'stretch.' "* In fact, logotherapy expands not only the concept of man, by including his higher aspirations, but also the visional field of the patient as to potentialities to feed and nurture his will to meaning. By the same token,

* *The New York Times*, November 26, 1975.

logotherapy immunizes the patient against the dehumanizing, mechanistic concept of man on which many a "shrink" is sold—in a word, it makes the patient "shrink-*resistant*."

The argument that one should not think too highly of man presupposes that it is dangerous to overrate him. But it is much more dangerous to underrate him, as has been pointed out by Goethe. Man, particularly the younger generation, may be corrupted by being underrated. Conversely, if I am cognizant of the higher aspirations of man—such as his will to meaning—I am also able to muster and mobilize them.

The will to meaning is not only a matter of faith but also a fact. Since I introduced the concept in 1949, it has been empirically corroborated and validated by several authors, using tests and statistics. The Purpose-in-Life (PIL) Test* devised by James C. Crumbaugh and Leonard T. Maholik, and Elisabeth S. Lukas's Logo-Test have been administered to thousands of subjects, and the computerized data leave no doubt that the will to meaning is real.

Similarly, research conducted by S. Kratochvil and I. Planova of the Department of Psychology of the University of Brno, Czechoslovakia produced evidence that "the will to meaning is really a specific need not reducible to other needs, and is in greater or smaller degree present in all human beings." The authors continue: "The relevance of the frustration of this need was documented also by case material, concerning neurotic and depressive patients. In some cases the frustration of the will to meaning had a

---

* Psychometric Affiliates, P.O. Box 3167, Munster, Indiana 46321.

relevant role as an etiological factor in the origin of the neurosis or of the suicidal attempt."

One might also consider the result of a survey published by the American Council on Education: among 171,509 students screened, the highest goal—held by 68.1 percent—was "developing a meaningful philosophy of life."* Another survey, of 7,948 students at forty-eight colleges, was conducted by Johns Hopkins University under the sponsorship of the National Institute of Mental Health. Of these, only 16 percent said their first goal was "making a lot of money," whereas 78 percent checked "finding a purpose and meaning to my life."† Parallel findings were collected by the University of Michigan: 1,533 working people were asked to rank various aspects of work in order of importance, and "good pay" came in a distant fifth. Small wonder that Joseph Katz of the State University of New York, reviewing some recent opinion polls, said that "the next wave of personnel entering industry will be interested in careers with meaning, not money."‡

Let us return for a moment to the research initiated by the National Institute of Mental Health. Seventy-eight percent of the students screened said their first goal was finding meaning to life—seventy-eight percent, which, as it happens, is exactly the percentage of Polish youngsters who regarded as their highest purpose in life something wholly different, namely, "to improve their living standard" (*Kurier*, August 8,

* Robert L. Jacobson, *The Chronicle of Higher Education* (Washington, D.C.: American Council on Education, January 10, 1972).
† *Los Angeles Times*, February 12, 1971.
‡Joseph Katz, in *Psychology Today*, Vol. 5, No. 1.

1973). Maslow's hierarchy of needs appears to apply here: first one must achieve a satisfactory standard of living and only then may he approach the task of finding a purpose and meaning in life, as the American students put it. The question is whether or not, if one wants to establish a good life, he has only to settle the socioeconomic situation (so that he can afford a psychoanalyst in order to settle the psychodynamic situation). I believe not. It goes without saying that someone who is ill wishes to become healthy, so health will seem to constitute his supreme goal in life. But in fact health is no more than a means to an end, a precondition for attaining whatever might be considered the real meaning in a given instance. In such a case it is mandatory first to inquire what is the end that stands behind the means. An appropriate method for such an inquiry may well be some sort of Socratic dialogue.

Maslow's motivation theory does not suffice here, for what is needed is not so much the distinction between higher and lower needs, but rather an answer to the question of whether individual goals are mere means, or meanings. In everyday life we are fully aware of this difference. If we were not, we wouldn't laugh at a comic strip that shows Snoopy complaining of a feeling of meaninglessness and emptiness—until Charlie Brown comes in with a bowl full of dog food, and Snoopy exclaims, "Ah Meaning!!" What makes us laugh is precisely the confusion of means and meaning: while food is certainly a necessary condition for survival, it is no sufficient condition to endow one's life with meaning and thus relieve the sense of meaninglessness and emptiness.

Maslow's distinction between higher and lower

needs does not take into account that when lower needs are *not* satisfied, a higher need, such as the will to meaning, may become most urgent. Just consider such situations as are met in death camps, or simply on deathbeds: who would deny that in such circumstances the thirst for meaning, even ultimate meaning, breaks through irresistibly?

As to deathbeds, this goes without saying. Less obvious might be what happened in the ghetto of Theresienstadt: A transport with about 1,000 young people was scheduled to leave the next morning. When the morning came, it turned out that over night the ghetto library had been burglarized. Each of the youngsters—who were doomed to death in the concentration camp of Auschwitz—had provided himself with a couple of books by his favorite poet or novelist or scientist, and had hidden the books in his rucksack. Who now would like to persuade me that Bertold Brecht was right when he proclaimed, in his *Dreigroschenoper,* "First comes feed and second, morals" *(Erst kommt das Fressen, dann kommt die Moral)?*

Yet as we have seen, not only extremity, but also affluence can trigger man's search for meaning—or as the case may be, it can frustrate his will to meaning. This holds for affluence in general and particularly for affluence in the form of leisure time. As both the satisfaction and the frustration of lower needs may challenge man to search for meaning, it follows that the need for meaning is independent of other needs. Hence, it can neither be reduced to them, nor deduced from them.

The will to meaning is not only a true manifestation of man's humanness, but also—as has been substantiated by Theodore A. Kotchen—a reliable criterion of mental health. This hypothesis is supported by James C. Crumbaugh, Sister Mary Raphael and Raymond R. Shrader, who measured the will to meaning and obtained the highest scores among well-motivated and successful professional and business populations. Conversely, lack of meaning and purpose is indicative of emotional maladjustment, as has been empirically evidenced by Elisabeth S. Lukas. To quote Albert Einstein, "The man who regards his life as meaningless is not merely unhappy but hardly fit for life." This is not only a matter of success and happiness, but also of survival. In the terminology of modern psychology, the will to meaning has "survival value." This was the lesson I had to learn in three years spent in Auschwitz and Dachau: *ceteris paribus* (other things being equal), those most apt to survive the camps were those oriented toward the future—toward a task, or a person, waiting for them in the future, toward a meaning to be fulfilled by them in the future.*

---

* It is true that if there was anything to uphold man in such an extreme situation as Auschwitz and Dachau, it was the awareness that life has a meaning to be fulfilled, albeit in the future. But meaning and purpose were only a necessary condition of survival, not a sufficient condition. Millions had to die in spite of their vision of meaning and purpose. Their belief could not save their lives, but it did enable them to meet death with heads held high. I therefore deemed it appropriate to pay tribute to them on the occasion of the inauguration of the Frankl Library and Memorabilia at the Graduate Theological Union in Berkeley, California, when I presented the custodian with a donation: a sample of soil and ashes I had brought with me from Auschwitz. "It is to commemorate," I said, "those who lived there as heros and died there as martyrs. Uncounted examples of such heroism and martyrdom bear witness to the

The same conclusion has since been reached by other authors of books on concentration camps, and also by psychiatric investigations concerning Japanese, North Korean and North Vietnamese prisoner-of-war camps. When I once had as students three American officers who had served long terms—up to seven years—in North Vietnamese POW camps, they too had found that the prisoners who felt there was something or someone waiting for them were the ones most likely to survive. The message—the legacy—is that survival depended on the direction to a "what for," or a "whom for." In a word, existence was dependent on "self-transcendence," a concept that I introduced into logotherapy as early as 1949. I thereby understand the primordial anthropological fact that being human is being always directed, and pointing, to something or someone other than oneself: to a meaning to fulfill or another human being to encounter, a cause to serve or a person to love. Only to the extent that someone is living out this self-transcendence of human existence, is he truly human or does he become his true self. He becomes so, not by concerning himself with his self's actualization, but by forgetting himself and giving himself, overlooking himself and focusing outward. Consider the eye, an analogy I am fond of invoking. When, apart from looking in a mirror, does the eye see anything of itself? An eye with a cataract may see something like a cloud, which is its

---

uniquely human potential to find, and fulfill, meaning even 'in extremis' and 'in ultimus'—in an extreme life situation such as Auschwitz and even in the face of one's death in a gas chamber. May from unimaginable suffering spring forth a growing awareness of life's unconditional meaningfulness."

cataract; an eye with glaucoma may see its glaucoma as a rainbow halo around the lights. A healthy eye sees nothing of itself—it is self-transcendent.

What is called self-actualization is, and must remain, the unintended effect of self-transcendence; it is ruinous and self-defeating to make it the target of intention. And what is true of self-actualization also holds for identity and happiness. It is the very "pursuit of happiness" that obviates happiness. The more we make it a target, the more widely we miss. This is most conspicuous when it comes to sexual happiness, to sexual "pleasure-seeking." Sexual neuroses are the result. The more a male patient wishes to demonstrate his potency, the more surely he is doomed to failure. The more a female patient wishes to demonstrate to herself that she is capable of orgasm, the more likely she is to wind up with frigidity. Here, let me just refer you to the chapter that deals explicitly with the clinical applications of logotherapy and its techniques ("Paradoxical Intention and Dereflection"), where the subject is elaborated, with pertinent case material to illustrate the point.

In a well-known experiment, reported by Carolyn Wood Sherif, group aggressions were built up in a group of young people. However, once they were united in the common task of dragging a carriage out of the mud, they simply "forgot" to live out their aggressions. Their will to meaning, one may say, had taken over! And I think that peace research, rather than confining itself to the rehash of clichés about aggressive potentials and the like, should zero in on the will to meaning, and take into account that what is true of individual men holds equally for mankind. Shouldn't the survival of humanity too be contingent on whether or not men arrive at a common denominator of meaning? Shouldn't it be contingent on whether or not people, and peoples, find a *common* meaning, become united in a common *will* to a common meaning?

I do not have the answer. I would be content if I knew that I asked the right question. Yet it would seem that in the final analysis there is hope for planetary survival only if nations can be united in confronting and committing themselves to a common task.

So far, one may say only that we are under way. But man's search for meaning—obviously—is a worldwide phenomenon of which our generation is witness, and why shouldn't this common search for meaning also lead up to a common goal and purpose?

A MEANING TO LIFE

So there is a will to meaning in man; but is there also a meaning to life? In other words, having dealt with the motivational-theoretical aspect of logotherapy, we now turn to "logo-theory"—i.e., logotherapy's theory of meaning. And to begin with, let us ask ourselves whether a logotherapist can impart meaning. I would say that, in the first place, he should see to it that meaning not be taken away—because this is precisely what is being done by reductionism. In the following chapters, as well as in other books of mine, numerous examples are cited.

Let me here just recall an incident that happened to me when I was thirteen years old. Once my science teacher walked up and down between the rows and taught the class that, in the final analysis, life was nothing but a combustion process, an oxidation process. I jumped up and, without asking permission as was customary at that time, threw him the question, "What meaning, then, does life have?" Of course, he could not answer, because he was a reductionist.

The question is, how do we help people in despair over the apparent meaninglessness of life. I said at the outset that values are disappearing because they are transmitted by traditions and we are facing a decay of traditions. Even so, I think it is still possible to find meanings. Reality presents itself always in the form of a specific concrete situation, and since each life situation is unique, it follows that also the meaning of a situation must be unique. Therefore it would not even be possible for meanings to be transmitted through traditions. Only values—which might be defined as universal meanings—can be affected by the decay of traditions.

One may say that instincts are transmitted through the genes, and values are transmitted through traditions, but that meanings, being unique, are a matter of personal discovery. They must be sought and found by oneself, and such discovery of unique meanings, as we now understand, will be possible even if all universal values disappear totally. To put it succinctly: the values are dead—long live the meanings.

But how is this discovery of meaning really enacted? It goes to the credit of James C. Crumbaugh to have pointed out that the business of finding meanings boils down to a process of Gestalt perception. I myself have come to see a difference, for in a Gestalt perception in the traditional sense of the term we are perceiving a figure against a background; in finding meaning, however, we are perceiving a possibility embedded in reality. Specifically, this is a possibility to do something about a situation confronting us, to change a reality, if need be. Since each situation is unique, with a meaning that is also necessarily unique, it now follows that the "possibility to do something about a situation" is unique also insofar as it is transitory. It has a "kairos" quality, which means that unless we use the opportunity to fulfill the meaning inherent and dormant in a situation, it will pass and be gone forever.

Yet it is only the possibilities—the opportunities to do something about reality—that are transitory. Once we have actualized the possibility offered by a situation, once we have fulfilled the meaning a situation holds, we have converted that possibility into a reality, and we have done so once *and forever!* Then it is no longer assailable by transitoriness. We have, as it were, rescued it into the past. Nothing and nobody can deprive and rob us of what we have safely delivered and deposited in the past. In the past, nothing is irretrievably and irrecoverably lost, but everything is permanently stored. Usually, to be sure, people see only the stubblefield of transitoriness—they do not see the full granaries into which they have brought in the harvest of their lives: the deeds done, the works created, the loves loved, the sufferings courageously gone through. In this sense we may understand what has been said of man, in Job: that he comes to his grave "like a shock of corn cometh in in his season."

As meanings are unique, they are ever changing. But they are never missing. Life is never lacking a meaning. To be sure, this is only understandable if we recognize that there is potential meaning to be found even beyond work and love. Certainly we are used to discovering meaning in creating a work or doing a deed, or in experiencing something or encountering someone. But we must never forget that we may also find meaning in life even when confronted with a hopeless situation as its helpless victim, when facing a fate that cannot be changed. For what then counts and matters is to bear witness to the uniquely human potential at its best, which is to transform a tragedy into a personal triumph, to turn one's predicament into a human achievement. When we are no longer able to change a situation—just think of an incurable disease, say, an inoperable cancer—we are challenged to change ourselves.

This is brought home most beautifully by the words of Yehuda Bacon, an Israeli sculptor who was imprisoned in Auschwitz when he was a young boy and after the war wrote a paper from which I would like to quote a passage: "As a boy I thought: 'I will tell them what I saw, in the hope that people will change for the better.' But people didn't change and didn't even want to know. It was much later that I really understood *the meaning of suffering*. It can have a meaning if it changes oneself for the better." He finally recognized the meaning of his suffering: he changed himself.

Changing oneself often means rising above oneself, growing beyond oneself. Nowhere will you find a more gripping illustration than in Leo Tolstoy's novel *The Death of Ivan Ilyich.** May I also draw your attention to the title of Elisabeth Kübler-Ross's recent book, *Death, the Final Stage of Growth,* a title that in this context is highly significant.

What I wanted to convey to you is the secret of life's unconditional meaningfulness, which owes to the third possibility of finding meaning in life, the possibility of investing meaning even in suffering and death. Seen in this light, it is fitting that in *The American Journal of Psychiatry* a statement is to be found to the effect that "unconditional faith in an unconditional meaning is Dr. Frankl's message." However, I think it is more than "faith." It is true, my conviction of that life is unconditionally meaningful began as an intuition. Small wonder: at that time I was a high school student. But since then the same conclusion has been reached on strictly empirical grounds. Let me just mention the names of Brown, Casciani, Crumbaugh, Dansart, Durlak, Kratochvil, Lukas, Lunceford, Mason, Meier, Murphy, Planova, Popielski, Richmond, Roberts, Ruch, Sallee, Smith, Yarnell and Young. These authors have evidenced by tests and statistics that in fact meaning is available to each and every person—regardless of sex or age, IQ or educational background, environment or character structure, or—last but not least—whether or not he is religious, and if he is, the denomination to which he may belong.

None of this alters the fact that conditions may vary

---

* In the chapter "Symptom or Therapy?" I tell of addressing the prisoners of San Quentin and, in this setting, quoting from *The Death of Ivan Ilyich.*

in the degree to which they make it easier or more difficult for an individual to find a meaning in his life or to fulfill the meaning of a given situation. Just consider the different societies and the different extents to which they promote or inhibit meaning fulfillment. In principle, nonetheless, the fact remains that meaning is available under any conditions, even the worst conceivable ones.

To be sure, a logotherapist cannot tell a patient what the meaning is, but he at least can show that *there is* a meaning in life, that it is available to everyone and, even more, that life retains its meaning under any conditions. It remains meaningful literally up to its last moment, up to one's last breath.

The trichotomy of meaning potentials I have presented exists in a hierarchy—and, remarkably enough, both the meanings and their hierarchy have been empirically corroborated by Elisabeth S. Lukas. When data obtained by tests and statistics were submitted to factoral analysis, evidence emerged in favor of my assumption that the meaning found in suffering belongs to a different dimension than the meanings found in work and love—or, to stick to the factoral-analytical terminology, it is located on an orthogonal axis.

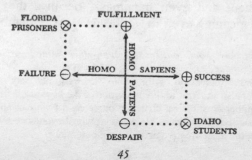

Usually, man is seen as the *homo sapiens,* the clever man who has know-how, who knows how to be a success, how to be a successful businessman or a successful playboy, that is, how to be successful in making money or in making love. The *homo sapiens* moves between the positive extreme of success and its negative counterpart, failure.

It is different with what I call the *homo patiens,** the suffering man, the man who knows how to suffer, how to mold even his sufferings into a human achievement. The *homo patiens* moves on an axis perpendicular to the success/failure axis of the *homo sapiens.* He moves on an axis which extends between the poles of fulfillment and despair. By fulfillment we understand fulfillment of one's self through the fulfillment of meaning, and by despair, despair over the apparent meaninglessness of one's life.

Only if we recognize that there are two different dimensions† involved is it possible to understand how on one hand we can meet people who in spite of success are caught in despair—just remember the Idaho students who attempted suicide in spite of their affluence—while on the other hand we come across people who in spite of failure have arrived at a sense of fulfillment and even happiness, because they have found meaning even in suffering. Just remember the

---

* Cf. my book *homo patiens: Versuch einer Pathodizee,* Vienna, Franz Deuticke, 1950.

† Really the dimension of the *homo patiens* is not only different from, but also superior to the dimension of the *homo sapiens.* It is a higher dimension, for by changing ourselves (if we can no longer change our fate), by rising above and growing beyond ourselves, we exercise the most creative of all human potentials.

two letters from which I quoted at the beginning. In conclusion, let me quote from two more letters I received, one from Frank E., who was Number 020640 in an American state prison: "I have found true meaning in my existence even here, in prison. I find purpose in my life, and this time I have left is just a short wait for the opportunity to do better, and to do more." And from another prisoner, Number 552022:

> Dear Dr. Frankl,
> During the past several months a group of inmates have been sharing your books and your tapes. Yes, one of the greatest meanings we can be privileged to experience is suffering. I have just begun to live, and what a glorious feeling it is. I am constantly humbled by the tears of my brothers in our group when they can see that they are even now achieving meanings they never thought possible. The changes are truly miraculous. Lives which heretofore have been hopeless and helpless now have meaning. Here in Florida's maximum security prison, some 500 yards from the electric chair, we are actualizing our dreams. It is near Christmas, but logotherapy was my Easter Morning. Out of the Calvary of Auschwitz has come our Easter Sunrise. From the barbed wire and chimney of Auschwitz rises the sun. . . . My, what a new day must be in store.
>
> Sincerely, Greg B.

I thank Greg for this letter, which I treasure because it is more than just a letter—I rather see therein a *document humain,* a document of humanness.

Determinism and Humanism: Critique of Pan-Determinism

THE TWO PERENNIAL PHILOSOPHICAL ISSUES, THE problem of body and mind, and the problem of free choice (or, as it might be expressed, determinism versus indeterminism), cannot be solved. But at least it is possible to identify the reason why they are unsolvable.

The body-mind problem can be reduced to the question: How is it possible to conceive of that unity in diversity which could be the definition of man? And who would deny that there is diversity in man? As Konrad Lorenz says: "The wall separating the two great incommensurables, the physiological and psychological, is unsurmountable. Even the extension of scientific research into the field of psychophysics did not bring us closer to the solution of the body-mind problem."* As to the hope that future research might bring a solution, Werner Heisenberg is equally pessimistic, contending that "we do not expect a direct way

---

* *Über tierisches und menschliches Verhalten*, Munich, 1965, pp. 362 and 372.

of understanding between bodily movements and psychological processes, for even in the exact sciences reality breaks down into separate levels."

In fact, we are living in an age of what I would call the pluralism of science, and the individual sciences depict reality in such different ways that the pictures contradict each other. However, it is my contention that the *contradictions do not contradict* the unity of reality. This holds true also of the human reality. In order to demonstrate this, let us recall that each science, as it were, cuts out a cross section of reality. Let us now follow the implications of this analogy from geometry:

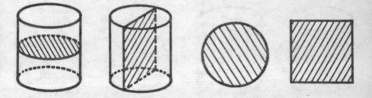

If we cut two orthogonal cross sections from a cylinder, the horizontal cross section represents the cylinder as a circle whereas the vertical cross section represents it as a square. But as we know, nobody has managed as yet to transform a circle into a square. Similarly, none has succeeded as yet in bridging the gap between the somatic and psychological aspects of the human reality. And, we may add, nobody is likely to succeed, because the *coincidentia oppositorum,* as Nicholas of Cusa has called it, is not possible within any cross section but only beyond all of them in the next higher dimension. It is no different with man. On the biological level, in the plane of biology, we are confronted with the somatic aspects of man, and on the psychological level, in the plane of psychology, with his psychological aspects. Thus, within the planes of both scientific approaches we are facing diversity but missing the unity in man, because this unity is available only in the human dimension. Only in the human dimension lies the *"unitas multiplex,"* as man has been defined by Thomas Aquinas. This unity is not really a unity *in* diversity but rather a unity *in spite of* diversity.

What is true of the oneness of man, also holds for his openness:

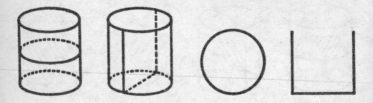

Going back to the cylinder, let us now imagine that it is not a solid but an open vessel, say, a cup. In that case, what will the cross sections be like? While the horizontal one still is a closed circle, in the vertical plane the cup is now seen as an open figure. But as soon as we realize that both figures are mere cross sections, the closedness of one figure is perfectly compatible with the openness of the other. Something analogous holds for man. He too is sometimes portrayed as if he were merely a closed system within which cause-effect relations, such as conditioned or unconditioned reflexes, are operant. On the other hand, being human is profoundly characterized as being open to the world, as Max Scheler, Arnold Gehlen and Adolf Portmann have shown. Or, as Martin Heidegger said, being human is "being in the world." What I have called the self-transcendence of existence denotes the fundamental fact that being human means relating to something, or someone, other than oneself, be it a meaning to fulfill, or human beings to encounter. And existence falters and collapses unless this self-transcendent quality is lived out.

That the self-transcendent quality of existence, the openness of being human, is touched by one cross section and missed by another is understandable. Closedness and openness have become compatible. And I think that the same holds true of freedom and determinism. There is determinism in the psychological dimension, and freedom in the noölogical dimension, which is the human dimension, the dimension of human phenomena. As to the body-mind problem, we wound up with the phrase "unity in spite of diversity." As to the problem of free choice, we are winding up with the phrase "freedom in spite of determinism." It parallels the phrase once coined by Nicolai Hartmann, "autonomy in spite of dependency."

As a human phenomenon, however, freedom is all too human. Human freedom is finite freedom. Man is not free from conditions. But he is free to take a stand in regard to them. The conditions do not completely condition him. Within limits it is up to him whether or not he succumbs and surrenders to the conditions. He may as well rise above them and by so doing open up and enter the human dimension. As I once put it: As a professor in two fields, neurology and psychiatry, I am fully aware of the extent to which man is subject to biological, psychological and sociological conditions. But in addition to being a professor in two fields I am a survivor of four camps—concentration camps, that is—and as such I also bear witness to the unexpected extent to which man is capable of defying and braving even the worst conditions conceivable. Sigmund Freud once said, "Let us attempt to expose a number of the most diverse people uniformly to hunger. With the increase of the imperative urge of hunger all individual differences will blur, and in their stead will appear the uniform expression of the one unstilled urge." In the concentration camps, however, the reverse was true. People became more diverse. The beast was unmasked—and so was the saint. The hunger was the same but people were different. In truth, calories do not count.

Ultimately, man is not subject to the conditions that confront him; rather, these conditions are subject to his decision. Wittingly or unwittingly, he decides whether he will face up or give in, whether or not he will let himself be determined by the conditions. Of course, it could be objected that such decisions are themselves determined. But it is obvious that this results in a *regressus in infinitum*. A statement by Magda B. Arnold epitomizes this state of affairs and lends itself as an apt conclusion of the discussion: "All choices are caused but they are caused by the chooser."*

Interdisciplinary research covers more than one

_____

* *The Human Person*, New York, 1954, p. 40.

cross section. It prevents one-sidedness. Regarding the problem of free choice, it prevents us from denying, on the one hand, the deterministic and mechanistic aspects of the human reality, or on the other hand, the human freedom to transcend them. This freedom is not denied by determinism but rather by what I am used to calling pan-determinism. In other words, the alternatives really are pan-determinism versus determinism, rather than determinism versus indeterminism. And as to Freud, he only espoused pan-determinism in theory. In practice, he was anything but blind to the human freedom to change, to improve, for instance, when he once defined the goal of psychoanalysis as giving "the patient's ego the freedom to choose one way or the other."*

Human freedom implies man's capacity to detach himself from himself. I like to illustrate this capacity with the following story: During World War I a Jewish army doctor was sitting together with his gentile friend, an aristocratic colonel, in a foxhole when heavy shooting began. Teasingly, the colonel said, "You are afraid, aren't you? Just another proof that the Aryan race is superior to the Semitic one." "Sure, I am afraid," was the doctor's answer. "But who is superior? If you, my dear colonel, were as afraid as I am, you would have run away long ago." What counts is not our fears and anxieties as such, but the attitude we adopt toward them. This attitude is freely chosen.

The freedom of choosing an attitude toward our psychological make-up even extends to the pathologi-

---

* *The Ego and the Id,* London, 1927, p. 72.

cal aspects of this make-up. Time and again, we psychiatrists meet patients whose response to their delusions is anything but pathological. I have met paranoiacs who, out of their delusional ideas of persecution, have killed their alleged enemies; but I have also met paranoiacs who have forgiven their supposed adversaries. The latter have not acted out of mental illness but rather reacted to this illness out of their humanness. To speak of suicide rather than homicide, there are cases of depression who commit suicide, and there are cases who manage to overcome the suicidal impulse for the sake of a cause or a person. They are too committed to commit suicide, as it were.

I for one am convinced that a psychosis such as a paranoia or an endogenous depression is somatogenic. More specifically, its etiology is biochemical—even though more often than not its exact nature could not yet be determined. (See Note 1 on p. 67.) Yet we are not justified in making fatalistic inferences. They would not be valid even in cases in which biochemistry is based on heredity. In context with the latter, for instance, I never weary of quoting Johannes Lange, who once reported a case of identical twin brothers. One brother wound up as a cunning criminal. The other wound up as a cunning criminologist. Being cunning might well be a matter of heredity. But becoming a criminal or a criminologist, as the case may be, is a matter of attitude. Heredity is no more than the material from which man builds himself. It is no more than the stones that are, or are not, refused and rejected by the builder. But the builder himself is not built of stones.

Even less than heredity does infancy univocally

determine the life course. A non-patient of mine once wrote me a letter in which she said: "I have suffered more from the thought that I should have complexes rather than from actually having them. Actually I would not trade my experiences for anything and believe a lot of good came out of them."*

Fatalism on the part of the psychiatrist is likely to reinforce fatalism on the part of the patient, which is characteristic of neurosis, anyway. And what is true of

* Moreover, early childhood experiences are not as decisive for the religious life as some psychologists have thought them to be. Least of all is it true that the concept of God is univocally determined by the father image. I had my staff at the Vienna Poliklinik Hospital screen the patients who visited its outpatient clinic in a single day. This screening showed that 23 patients had a positive father image, 13 a negative one. But only 16 of the subjects with a positive father image and only 2 of the subjects with a negative father image had allowed themselves to be fully determined by these images in their religious development. Half of the total number screened developed their religious concepts independently of their father image. A poor religious life cannot always be traced back to the impact of a negative father image. Nor does even the worst father image necessarily prevent one from establishing a sound relation to God (Viktor E. Frankl, *The Will to Meaning*, New York and Cleveland, 1969, p. 136f). The promise that "the truth will make you free" must not be interpreted as if being truly religious were a guarantee of being free from neurosis. Conversely, however, freedom from neurosis does not guarantee a truly religious life. Three years ago, I had an opportunity to discuss this issue with a prior who ran a Benedictine monastery in Mexico and insisted that the monks should undergo strictly Freudian psychoanalysis. The outcome? Only 20 percent stayed in the monastery. I wonder how few people would have become, and remained, psychiatrists if they too had been screened for neurotic flaws. Let him among you who is without neurotic flaws be the first to cast a stone at me, be he a theologian or a psychiatrist.

psychiatry also holds for sociatry. Pan-determinism serves the criminal as an alibi: it is the mechanisms within him that are blamed. Such an argument, however, proves to be self-defeating. If the defendant alleges that he really was not free and responsible when he committed his crime, the judge may claim the same when passing sentence.

Actually, criminals, at least once the judgment has been passed, do not wish to be regarded as mere victims of psychodynamic mechanisms or conditioning processes. As Scheler once pointed out, man has a *right* to be considered guilty and to be punished. To explain his guilt away by looking at him as the victim of circumstances also means taking away his human dignity. I would say that it is a prerogative of man to become guilty. To be sure, it also is his responsibility to overcome guilt. This is what I told the prisoners of San Quentin in California, whom I once addressed at the request of the prison's director. Joseph B. Fabry, an editor at the University of California, accompanied me and afterward related to me how these prisoners, who were the toughest criminals in California, had reacted to my address. One prisoner said, "The psychologists (in contrast to Frankl) always asked us about our childhood and the bad things in the past. Always the past—it's like a millstone around our necks." And then he added, "Most of us don't even come any more to hear psychologists speak. I only came because I read that Frankl had been a prisoner, too."*

Carl Rogers once arrived at "an empirical definition

---

* Joseph B. Fabry, *The Pursuit of Meaning*, Boston, 1968, p. 24.

of what constitutes 'freedom.' "* After a student of his, W. L. Kell, had studied 151 adolescent delinquents it turned out that their behavior could not be predicted on the basis of the family climate, educational or social experiences, neighborhood or cultural influences, health history, hereditary background, or any of the like. By far the best predictor was the degree of self-understanding, correlating .84 with later behavior. It would seem that self-understanding in this context implies self-detachment, detachment from oneself. The capacity of self-detachment, however, is crippled by pan-determinism.

Let us turn determinism against pan-determinism. That is, let us attempt a strictly causal explanation of the latter: Let us ask ourselves what are the causes of pan-determinism. I would say that it is lack of discrimination that causes pan-determinism. On the one hand, causes are confounded with reasons. On the other hand, causes are confounded with conditions. What, then, is the difference between causes and reasons? If you cut onions you weep—your tears have a cause. But you have no reason to weep. But if a loved one dies, you have reason to weep. If you do rock climbing and arrive at a height of 10,000 feet you may have to cope with a feeling of oppression and anxiety. This may stem from either a cause or a reason. Lack of oxygen may be the cause. But if you know that you are badly equipped or poorly trained, anxiety has a reason.

Being human has been defined as "being in the world." The world includes reasons and meanings.

---

*"Discussion," *Existential Inquiries*. Vol. 1, No. 2, 1960, pp. 9–13.

But reasons and meanings are excluded if you conceive of man as a closed system. What is left is causes and effects. The effects are represented by conditioned reflexes or responses to stimuli. The causes are represented by conditioning processes or drives and instincts. Drives and instincts push but reasons and meanings pull. If you conceive of man in terms of a closed system you notice only forces that push but no motives that pull. Consider the front doors of any American hotel. From inside the lobby you notice only the sign "push." The sign "pull" is visible only from without. Man has doors as does the hotel. He is no closed monad, and psychology degenerates into some sort of monadology unless it recognizes his openness to the world. This openness of existence is reflected by its self-transcendence. (See Note 2 on p. 68.) The self-transcendent quality of the human reality in turn is reflected in the "intentional" quality of human phenomena, as Franz Brentano and Edmund Husserl term it. Human phenomena refer and point to "intentional objects."* Reasons and meanings represent such objects. They are the logos for which the psyche is reaching out. If psychology is to be worthy of its name it has to recognize both halves of this name, the logos as well as the psyche.

When the self-transcendence of existence is denied, existence itself is distorted. It is reified. Being is reduced to a mere thing. Being human is de-personalized. And, what is most important, the subject is made into an object. This is due to the fact that it is the characteristic of a subject that it relates to objects.

* Herbert Spiegelberg, *The Phenomenological Movement*, Vol. 2, 1960, p. 721.

And it is a characteristic of man that he relates to intentional objects in terms of values and meanings which serve as reasons and motives. If self-transcendence is denied and the door to meanings and values is closed, reasons and motives are replaced by conditioning processes, and it is up to the "hidden persuaders" to do the conditioning, to manipulate man. It is reification that opens the door to manipulation. And vice versa. If one is to manipulate human beings he first has to reify them, and, to this end, indoctrinate them along the lines of pan-determinism. "Only by dispossessing autonomous man," says B. F. Skinner, "can we turn the real causes of human behavior—from the inaccessible to the manipulable."* I quite simply think, first of all, that conditioning processes are not the real causes of human behavior; secondly, that the real cause is something accessible, provided that the humanness of human behavior is not denied on *a priori* grounds; and, thirdly, that the humanness of human behavior cannot be revealed unless we recognize that the real "cause" of a given individual's behavior is not a cause but, rather, a reason.

Beyond Freedom and Dignity. New York: Alfred A. Knopf, 1971. Ludwig von Bertalanffy observes: "The expanding economy of the 'affluent society' could not subsist without such manipulation. Only by manipulating humans ever more into Skinnerian rats, robots, buying automata, homeostatically adjusted conformers and opportunists can this great society follow its progress toward ever increasing gross national product. The concept of man as robot was both an expression of and a powerful motive force in industrialized mass society. It was the basis for behavioral engineering in commercial, economic, political, and other advertising and propaganda." ("General System Theory and Psychiatry," in Silvano Arieti, ed., *American Handbook of Psychiatry,* Vol. 3, pp. 70 and 71.)

Causes are confused not only with reasons but also with conditions. In a way, however, causes are conditions. They are sufficient conditions in contrast to conditions in the strict sense of necessary conditions. Incidentally, there are not only necessary conditions but also what I would call possible conditions. By this I mean releases and triggers. So-called psychosomatic diseases, for example, are not caused by psychological factors—that is to say, they are not psychogenic as are neuroses. Rather, psychosomatic diseases are somatic diseases that have been triggered off by psychological factors.

A sufficient condition is sufficient to create and engender a phenomenon: i.e., the phenomenon is determined by such a cause not only in its essence but also in its existence. By contrast, a necessary condition is a precondition. It is a prerequisite. There are cases of mental retardation, for example, that are due to a hypofunction of the thyroid gland. If such a patient is given thyroid extract his I.Q. improves and increases. Does that mean that spirit is nothing but thyroid substance, as said in a book I once had to review? I would rather say that thyroid substance is "nothing but" a necessary condition which the author confounded with a sufficient condition. For a change, let us turn to a hypofunction of the adrenocortical glands. I myself have published two papers based on laboratory research to the effect that there are cases of depersonalization resulting from the hypofunction of the adrenocortical glands. If such a patient is given desoxycorticosterone acetate he again feels like a person. The sense of selfhood is restored. Does that mean that the self is nothing but desoxycorticosterone acetate?

Here we reach the point at which pan-determinism turns into reductionism. Indeed, it is the lack of discrimination between causes and conditions that allows reductionism to deduce a human phenomenon from, and reduce it to, a subhuman phenomenon. However, in being derived from a subhuman phenomenon, the human phenomenon is turned into a mere epiphenomenon.

Reductionism is the nihilism of today. It is true that Jean-Paul Sartre's brand of existentialism hinges on the pivots "Being and Nothingness," but the lesson to be learned from existentialism is a hyphenated nothingness, namely, the no-thingness of the human being. A human being is not one thing among other things. Things determine each other. Man, however, determines himself. Rather, he decides whether or not he lets himself be determined, be it by the drives and instincts that push him, or the reasons and meanings that pull him.

The nihilism of yesterday taught nothingness. Reductionism now is preaching nothing-but-ness. Man is said to be nothing but a computer or a "naked ape." It is perfectly legitimate to use the computer as a model, say, for the functioning of our central nervous system. The *analogia entis* extends and is valid down to the computer. However, there are also dimensional differences which are disregarded and neglected by reductionism. Consider, for example, the typically reductionist theory of conscience according to which this uniquely human phenomenon is nothing but the result of conditioning processes. The behavior of a dog that has wet the carpet and slinks under the couch with its tail between its legs does not manifest conscience but something I would rather call anticipatory anxiety—specifically, the fearful expectation of punishment. This might well be the result of conditioning processes. It has nothing to do with conscience, however, because true conscience has nothing to do with the expectation of punishment. As long as a man is still motivated either by the fear of punishment or by the hope of reward—or, for that matter, by the wish to appease the superego—conscience has not had its say as yet.

Lorenz was cautious enough to speak of "moral-*analoges* Verhalten bei Tieren"—behavior in animals that is *analogous* to moral behavior in man. Reductionists recognize no qualitative difference between the two. They deny that any uniquely human phenomenon exists, and this they do, not on empirical grounds as one might assume, but on an *a priori* basis. They insist that there is nothing in man that cannot be found in other animals. Or, to vary a well-known dictum, *nihil est in homine, quod non prius fuerit in animalibus.*

In a favorite story of mine, a rabbi was consulted by two parishioners. One contended that the other's cat had stolen and eaten five pounds of butter, which the other denied. "Bring me the cat," the rabbi ordered. They brought him the cat. "Now bring me scales." They brought him scales. "How many pounds of butter did you say the cat has eaten?" he asked. "Five pounds, rabbi," was the answer. Thereupon the rabbi put the cat on the scales and it weighed exactly five pounds. "Now I have the butter," the rabbi said, "but where is the cat?" This is what happens when eventually the reductionists rediscover in man all the conditioned reflexes, conditioning processes, innate releasing mechanisms and whatever else they have been seeking. "Now we have it," they say, like the rabbi, "but where is man?"

The devastating impact of an indoctrination along the lines of reductionism must not be underrated. Here I confine myself to quoting from a study by R. N. Gray and associates on 64 physicians, 11 of them psychiatrists. The study showed that during medical school cynicism as a rule increases while humanitarianism decreases. Only after completion of medical studies is this trend reversed, but unfortunately not in all subjects.* Ironically, the author of the paper which reports these results himself defines *man* as "an adaptive control system" and *values* as "homeostatic restraints in a stimulus-response process."† According to another reductionist definition, values are nothing but reaction formations and defense mechanisms. Such interpretations, needless to say, are likely to undermine and erode the appreciation of values.

As an example of what happens, a young American couple returned from Africa, where they had served as Peace Corps volunteers, completely fed up. At the outset they had had to participate in mandatory group sessions led by a psychologist who played a game

* "An Analysis of Physicians' Attitudes of Cynicism and Humanitarianism before and after Entering Medical Practice," *Journal of Medical Education,* Vol. 40, 1955, p. 760.
† Joseph Wilder, "Values and Psychotherapy," *American Journal of Psychotherapy,* Vol. 23, 1969, p. 405.

somewhat as follows: "Why did you join the Peace Corps?" "We wanted to help people less privileged." "So you must be superior to them." "In a way." "So there must be in you, in your unconscious, a need to prove to yourself that you are superior." "Well, I never thought of it that way, but you are a psychologist, you certainly know better." The group was indoctrinated to interpret their idealism and altruism as mere hang-ups. Even worse, the volunteers were constantly after each other with their own "what's *your* hidden motive" game. Here we are dealing with an instance of what I would call hyperinterpretation.

A recent study by Edith Weisskopf-Joelson and associates shows that the value that ranks highest among American college students is "self-interpretation."* Thus the cultural climate that prevails in the United States adds to the danger of self-interpretation becoming not only an obsession, as was the case with the Peace Corps volunteers, but even a *collective obsessive neurosis*. "Ex-patients analyze their motives in all situations," says E. Becker, "when they feel anxious: 'this must be penis-envy, this must be incestuous attraction, castration fear, Oedipal rivalry, polymorphous perversity,' and so on."†

Thus far we have discussed causes over against reasons and necessary conditions over against sufficient conditions. However, there is a third discrimination we have to consider. What is usually understood by "sufficient conditions" is efficient causes as op-

---

* "Relative Emphasis on Nine Values by a Group of College Students," *Psychological Reports,* Vol. 24, 1969, p. 299.
† *The Denial of Death.* New York, Free Press, 1974, p. 272.

posed to final causes. Now my contention is that final causes, or for that matter meanings and purposes, are perceptible and only to a scientific approach that is appropriate to them. The pan-determinist who contends that there are no meanings and purposes is like a man "who would study organic existence," to quote Johann Wolfgang von Goethe. He

> First drives out the soul with stern persistence;
> Then the parts in his hand he may hold and class,
> But the spiritual link is lost, alas!
> *Encheireisin naturae,* this Chemistry names,
> Nor knows how herself she banters and blames!
>
> *Faust,* Part I

There is a "missing link" indeed. Meaning is missing in the world as described by many a science. This, however, does not imply that the world is void of meaning, but only that many a science is blind to it. Meaning is scotomized by many a science. It is not demonstrated by every scientific approach; it is not touched by every "cross section," to stick to our simile. Consider a curve that lies in a vertical plane.

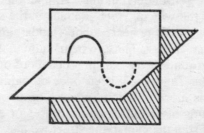

What is left of this line in a horizontal plane is no more than three points, isolated points, disconnected points,

points without a meaningful connection between them. The meaningful connections lie above and below the horizontal plane. Might it not be the same with those events which science sees as random, for example, chance mutations? And is it not conceivable that there is a hidden meaning, a higher or a deeper meaning that eludes the cross section because it lies above or below it as do the higher and the lower parts of the curve? (See Note 3, p. 69.) The fact remains that not everything can be explained in meaningful terms. But what now can be explained is at least the reason why this is *necessarily* the case.

If this is true of meaning, how much more does it hold for ultimate meaning. *The more comprehensive the meaning, the less comprehensible it is.* Infinite meaning is necessarily beyond the comprehension of a finite being. (See Note 4, p. 70.) Here is the point at which science gives up and wisdom takes over. Blaise Pascal once said, *"Le coeur a ses raisons, que la raison ne connait point"* (the heart has reasons that reason does not know). There is, indeed, what is called the wisdom of the heart.* Or one may call it the ontological self-understanding. A phenomenological analysis of the way in which the man in the street, out of the wisdom of the heart, understands himself, may teach us that there is more to being human than being the battleground of the clashing claims of ego, id and superego, as Fulton J. Sheen once mockingly put it, and there is more to being human than being a pawn and plaything of conditioning processes or drives and instincts. From the man in the street we may learn that

---

*" *In praecordiis sapientiam me doces.*"

being human means being confronted continuously with situations which are each at once chance and challenge, giving us a chance to fulfill ourselves by meeting the challenge to fulfill its meaning. Each situation is a call, first to listen, and then to respond.

And now the point is reached at which the circle is closed. We departed from determinism as a limitation of freedom and have arrived at humanism as an expansion of freedom. Freedom is part of the story and half of the truth. Being free is but the negative aspect of the whole phenomenon whose positive aspect is being responsible. Freedom may degenerate into mere arbitrariness unless it is lived in terms of responsibleness. That is why I would recommend that the Statue of Liberty on the East Coast be supplemented by a Statue of Responsibility on the West Coast.

NOTE 1: To a member of the medical profession, this is no unfamiliar state of affairs; how many among the diseases confronting a physician are of unknown origin—just consider cancer. Anyway, a psychosis is a matter of the bodily system's biochemistry. However, what the patient makes of his psychosis is entirely the property of his human personality. The psychosis that afflicts him is biochemical, but how he reacts to it, what he invests in it, the content with which he fills it—all this is his personal creation, is the human work into which he has molded his suffering. It is the way he has bestowed this suffering with meaning. While a psychosis is not meaningful in itself, it may be made meaningful by what the patient does about it—by the remaining and enduring inner growth he derives from it.

Edith Weisskopf-Joelson has hypothesized that "the paranoiac has an especially strong need for a consistent philosophy of life, and he develops his delusions as a substitute for such a philosophy" ("Paranoia and the Will-to-Meaning," *Existential Psychiatry*, I, 1966, 316–20). In other words, paranoia is "caused by the search for meaning," as she has put it. However, I see it differently. If we take it for granted that paranoia is sometimes associated with a *hypertrophy of meaning*, such a hypertrophy does not constitute the etiology of the psychosis but rather its symptomatology. Similarly, another form of psychosis, endogenous depression, is sometimes associated with a *hypotrophy of meaning*, but the patient's blindness to meaning is not the cause of his depression but its symptom. Of course, this statement only holds for this particular type of (endogenous) depression, which in the final analysis is as much organically caused, although in a different sense, as paranoia. In plain words: the patient suffering from *endogenous* depression is prevented by his psychosis from seeing any meaning in his life, whereas the patient suffering from a *neurotic* depression may have become depressed because he could not see a meaning in his life.

The fact remains that the primary origin of psychoses is of some biochemical nature.

NOTE 2: One might argue that, in contrast to Freudian psychoanalysis, Adlerian "individual psychology" does pay due tribute to self-transcendence. In fact, Adlerian psychology views man as a being directed to goals rather than driven by drives, but the goals, upon closer scrutiny, do not actually transcend man's self or his psyche. Rather, they are conceived of as *intrapsychic,* insofar as man's strivings are, in the final analysis, seen as mere devices to come to terms with his feelings of inferiority and insecurity.

NOTE 3: It is perfectly legitimate for molecular biologist Jacques Monod to argue that all life results from the interaction of mutations and selection. In *Chance and Necessity* he writes that "Pure chance, only chance" is at the root of evolution. But he is mistaken when he continues, "the idea of chance is the only one conceivable, because it is the only one compatible with the facts of observation and experience. And nothing permits us to suppose that our conceptions on this point will have to or even be able to be revised." This no longer has anything to do with empirical science, but is an insistence based on personal philosophy, his private ideology. What he does at that moment is deliberately to lock himself into the dimension of biology and, even worse, deny on sheerly *a priori* grounds that other dimensions, higher dimensions, may exist. A scientist may stick to his science and stay in one dimension, but he should also remain open, keep his science open, at least to the *possibility* of another, higher dimension.

As I have said, a higher dimension is higher in that it is more inclusive. If, for example, you take a cube and project it vertically so that it becomes a square, then you may say that this square is included in the cube. Anything occurring in the square will be contained as well in the cube, and nothing that takes place in the square can contradict what occurs in the higher dimension of the cube. The higher dimension does not exclude; it includes. And between the higher and lower dimensions of truth there can be only inclusiveness.

It would be appropriate if a biologist, instead of selling his own belief, or disbelief, under the guise of science, just declared that within the plane of biology nothing such as a higher or ultimate meaning and purpose shows up. There is no evidence of teleology, he might say. But unless he is a reductionist he will not exclude the possibility that within the next higher dimension teleology may well obtain. Our scientists need to have more than knowledge: they need to have wisdom as well. And wisdom I define as knowledge plus the awareness of its limitations.

NOTE 4: The concept of such a *meta-meaning* is not necessarily theistic. Even the concept of God need not necessarily be theistic. When I was fifteen years old or so I came up with a definition of God to which, in my old age, I come back more and more. I would call it an operational definition. It reads as follows: God is the partner of your most intimate soliloquies. Whenever you are talking to yourself in utmost sincerity and ultimate solitude—he to whom you are addressing yourself may justifiably be called God. Such a definition avoids the dichotomy between atheistic and theistic Weltanschauungs. The difference between them emerges only later on, when the irreligious person insists that his soliloquies are just that, monologues with himself, and the religious person interprets his as real dialogues with someone else. I think that what counts first and more than anything else is the utmost sincerity and honesty. If God really exists he certainly is not going to argue with the irreligious persons because they mistake him for their own selves and misname him.

Critique of Pure Encounter: How Humanistic Is "Humanistic Psychology"?

WHAT AT PRESENT SEEMS TO BE NEEDED IN PSYCHOL-ogy more than anything else is for psychotherapy to enter the human dimension, the dimension of the human phenomena. Let us therefore ask whether this step has really been taken by what has come to be called the "humanistic psychology" movement. Although logotherapy is said to have "joined" this movement (Charlotte Bühler and Melanie Allen, 1972), it may, for heuristic reasons, be wise to detach logotherapy from humanistic psychology in order to take a critical vantage and critically to comment on it. We will place special emphasis on that aspect of the movement which hinges on the concept of encounter, since it is particularly this concept which has been so misunderstood, not to say misused, by many of those who advocate it.

Actually, the concept of encounter has been derived from existentialist rather than humanistic psychological literature. It was introduced by Martin Buber,

Ferdinand Ebner, and Jacob L. Moreno, whose contribution to existentialist thought boils down to an interpretation of existence in terms of coexistence. In this context, encounter is understood as a relationship between an I and a Thou—a relationship which, by its very nature, can be established only on the human and personal level.

The fact remains that in this view something has been left out, and it is no more or less than a whole dimension. This becomes understandable when we remember and apply the theory of language propounded by Karl Bühler. His is the discrimination of a threefold function of language. First, language allows the speaker to express himself—it serves as a vehicle of self-expression. Second, language is an appeal addressed by the speaker to the person to whom he speaks. And third, language always represents something, that "something" of which one speaks. In other words, whenever one sets out to speak he is (a) expressing himself while (b) addressing himself "to" someone else; however, unless he also speaks "of" something, it is really not justified to call this process "language." What we then have to deal with is rather a type of pseudo-language which, indeed, is no more than a mode of self-expression (and sometimes even lacks the appeal to a partner). There are schizophrenics whose way of talking may well be interpreted as such a "language," expressing only mood, but no longer referring to reality.*

What is true of language also holds for coexistence

---

* Early in the thirties I demonstrated a pertinent case in the *Gesellschaft für Angewandte Psychologie* of Vienna.

and encounter, inasmuch as here too the third aspect of interhuman and interpersonal communication has to be considered and taken into account. It is this aspect for which phenomenology along the lines of Brentano and Husserl has coined the term "intentional referent" (Spiegelberg, 1972). And all the potential intentional referents together, all those objects to which language refers, all those objects which are "meant" by two subjects communicating with one another, form a structured whole, a world of "meaning," and this "cosmos" of meanings is what may aptly be called the "logos." From this it can be seen that any psychology that shuts out the meanings, cuts the human being off from his "intentional referents," castrates itself, as it were. A psychology deserving of its name has to pay due tribute to both halves of that name—the logos as well as the psyche.

Buber and Ebner not only discovered the central place that encounter occupies in the life of the human spirit but also defined this life as basically a dialogue between an I and a Thou. However, it is my contention that no true dialogue is possible unless the dimension of the logos has been entered. I would say a dialogue without the logos, lacking the direction to an intentional referent, is really a mutual monologue, merely mutual self-expression. What is missed is that quality of the human reality which I call "self-transcendence" (Frankl, 1962, 1966), denoting the fact that being human basically means relating, and being directed, to something other than oneself. The "intentionality" of cognitive acts, which has always been much emphasized by the phenomenological school of thought, forms just one aspect of the more comprehensive human phenomenon, the self-transcendence of human existence. A dialogue that is restricted to mere self-expression does not participate in the self-transcendent quality of the human reality. True encounter is a mode of coexistence that is open to the logos, allowing the partners to transcend themselves toward the logos, and even promoting such mutual self-transcendence.

One should not overlook nor forget, however, that self-transcendence means reaching out not only for a meaning to fulfill but also for another human being, another person, to love. To be sure, love goes beyond encounter inasmuch as the latter moves on the human, the former on the personal level. Encounter in the broader sense of the word makes us realize the humanness of the partner, whereas loving him shows us more—his essential uniqueness. This uniqueness is the constitutive characteristic of personhood. As to self-transcendence, however, it is equally implied whether man transcends himself by meaning fulfillment or loving encounter: in the first case, an impersonal logos is involved; in the second, a personal logos—an incarnated logos, so to speak.

In contrast to the traditional concept of encounter developed by Buber and Ebner, the conventional concept propounded by the bulk of literature in the field of humanistic psychology still adheres to an old-fashioned psychology which really is a monadology, seeing man as a monad without windows that would allow for self-transcendent relationships. Thereby the concept of encounter is vulgarized. Rather than being really humanistic, it is mechanistic, and so it comes to pass that what Peter R. Hofstätter of Hamburg University once aptly called "libido hydraulics" still permeates much of the encounter group movement.

The following case may serve as a flagrant example. A lady who had joined an encounter group was very excited and angry with her former husband, from whom she had been divorced. The group leader invited her to stab a balloon in order to vent her aggression and anger. In other words, the balloon was to replace the real object, namely, the husband. However, one could say as well that the purpose of letting her "act out" was to substitute the balloon for the wife as the *subject* of an explosion. After all, the purpose was to prevent her from "exploding." And, after acting out, she might in fact have felt relief. But are we really justified in assuming that the alleged relief after the presumed release of aggression is an authentic experience? What is the proof that it is not rather the result of inadvertent indoctrination, an indoctrination precisely along the lines of an outdated concept of man that is entirely mechanistic? Acting out has not changed anything: the reasons for being angry are still there! Basically, a person cares first whether or not there is a reason to be angry, and only peripherally for his own emotions in terms of anger of whatever other reaction he may show. But a mechanistic concept of man as it underlies a treatment like the one outlined above induces the patient to interpret himself in terms of the "libido hydraulics" operant within him. By so doing, it makes him forget that, after all, a human being may as well do something about a given situation; he may take his stand and he may even choose his attitude toward his own emotions, aggressions, etc. This "human potential" at its best should be allotted a central place in a truly humanistic concept of man. A therapeutic practice based on such a theory would see to it that the awareness of this potential is promoted in the patient. It is the awareness of man's freedom to change something in the world for the better, if possible, and to change himself for the better, if necessary. Again to take up the case of the divorced woman— what about her choosing that attitude called "reconciliation," be it that she reconciles to her husband if possible, or, if need be, that she reconciles to her fate as a divorced wife and then goes ahead and turns this predicament into an accomplishment on the human level! Well, wouldn't we deny our patient this possibility thus to rise above her predicament, to grow beyond it, and eventually to mold her negative experience into something positive, constructive, creative; wouldn't we block such a possibility in the patient if we made her believe what a neurotic is prone to believe anyway, namely, that she is the pawn and victim of outer influences or inner circumstances? Or, to stick to the case at hand, that she is dependent on a husband who will or will not reconcile to her, or dependent on aggressions that will or will not give way and be vented, say, after she stabs a balloon?

For a change, let us take up grief rather than anger and ask ourselves what might be the reaction of a person who is mourning a loved one and is offered a tranquilizer: "Closing one's eyes before reality does not do away with reality. That I fall asleep and am no longer conscious of the death of someone I love does not do away with the fact that he is dead. This is the only thing I care about: whether he is alive or dead— and not whether I am upset or not!" In other words, what he does care for is not whether he is happy or unhappy but whether there is a reason to be happy or unhappy. Wilhelm Wundt's system has been criticized as a "psychology without psyche." This has long been overcome, but there is still around what I would call a "psychology without logos," a psychology which interprets human behavior not as being induced by reasons that are out there in the world, but rather as resulting from causes that are operant within one's own psyche (or soma). But, as I have pointed out, causes are not the same as reasons. If you feel unhappy and have a whiskey it "causes" your unhappiness to disappear, but the reason to be unhappy will still remain. The same holds for the tranquilizer, which equally cannot change one's fate or bereavement. But again, what about changing one's attitude, turning a predicament into an achievement on the human level? There is certainly no place for anything like this in a psychology that divorces man from the world—the world in which alone his actions can have reasons, and in which even his suffering may have a meaning. A psychology that sees man as a closed system in which an interplay of dynamics is operant, rather than as a being reaching out for a meaning to crown his existence—such a psychology necessarily must deprive man of his capacity to turn tragedy into triumph.

The trouble really starts with the concept of aggression, be it the biological concept along the lines of Konrad Lorenz, or the psychological concept along the lines of Sigmund Freud. These concepts are inappropriate and inadequate because they totally neglect intentionality as an intrinsic human phenomenon. In fact, there is no such thing as aggression within my psyche, seeking an outlet and forcing me, its "mere victim," to search for objects that lend themselves to the business of acting it out. On the human level—i.e., as a human being—I do not harbor a fixed amount of aggression and then direct it to a convenient target; what I really do is something different: I hate! Be it that I hate something or someone. To be sure, hating something is more meaningful than hating someone (the creator, or "owner," of what I hate), because if I do not hate him personally, I may help him to overcome what I hate in him. I may even love him, in spite of what I hate in him. However this might be, hate as well as love is a human phenomenon—in contrast to aggression—and both are human because they are intentional: I have a reason to hate something, and I have a reason to love somebody. In contrast, aggression is due to causes. These causes may be of a psychological or physiological nature. As to the latter possibility, just consider Hess's classical experiments in which he could arouse aggression by electrically stimulating certain centers in the brains of cats.

What an injustice it would be to hypothesize that those who joined the resistance movement against National Socialism were merely pursuing the abreaction of aggressive impulses that just had happened, as it were, to be turned against Adolf Hitler. In actual fact, most of them did not really intend to fight a man called Adolf Hitler but rather the system called National Socialism.

Today aggression has become a topical—not to say fashionable—subject dealt with in congresses and conferences. What is even more important, so-called peace research has zeroed in on aggression. However,

I believe that peace research is doomed to failure as long as it leans on this inhuman and impersonal concept. Of course, aggressive impulses do exist in man, whether we interpret them as a heritage from our subhuman ancestors or as something reactive, along the lines of psychodynamic theories. On the human level, however, aggressive impulses never exist *per se* in a person, but always as something toward which he has to take a stand, toward which he has taken a stand all along, whether he has chosen to identify himself with them or to detach himself from them.* What matters in a given case is the personal attitude toward the impersonal aggressive impulses rather than the impulses themselves.

This is paralleled by suicidal impulses. There is no point, for instance, in trying to measure them. In the final analysis, the suicidal risk does not depend on the strength of the suicidal impulses within the person but on his response, as a person, to these impulses; and his reaction in turn will basically depend on whether or not he sees in survival something meaningful—even if painful. To be sure, there is also a test that does not pretend to measure the suicidal impulses themselves, but evaluates the incomparably more decisive factor, which is the personal attitude toward them. I developed the test early in the thirties, and described it first in English in *The Doctor and the Soul* (Frankl, 1955, p. 282).

Peace research, we may say, is concerned with the

---

* This is a manifestation of the uniquely human capacity of self-detachment. Self-transcendence is manifested by the aforementioned fact that hate, in contrast to aggression, is intentional.

survival of mankind as a whole. But it is handicapped by the fatalism that results from staring at the aggressive impulses rather than appealing to the human capacity to take a personal stand in regard to them. Thus, the aggressive impulses are made into an alibi, an excuse for hate. Man will not cease to hate as long as he is taught that it is the impulses and mechanisms that do the hating. It is he who does it! What is even more important, the concept of "aggressive potentials" makes people believe that aggression can be channeled. In fact, behavioral researchers of Konrad Lorenz' team have found that attempts to deflect aggression to unimportant objects and abreact it through harmless activities only provokes and usually reinforces it.

The difference between aggression and hate is paralleled by that between sex and love: I am driven to a partner by my sex drive. On the other hand, on the human level, I love the partner because, as I feel, I have a lot of reasons to do so; and sexual intercourse with her is an expression of love, its "incarnation," so to speak. On the subhuman level, to be sure, I would see her as no more than just an object of libido cathexis—a more or less fit means to get rid of surplus sperma. Sexual activity with such an attitude is often described by our patients as "masturbating on a woman." In so speaking, they implicitly contrast it with the normal approach to the partner, with sexual behavior on the human and personal level. There they no longer would see the partner as an "object" but rather as another subject. This would preclude their regarding the other human being as a mere means to an end—any end. On the human level, one no longer "uses" the partner but encounters him on a man-to-man basis. On the personal level, he meets the partner on a person-to-person basis, and this means that he loves the partner. Encounter preserves the humanness of the partner; love discovers his uniqueness as a person.

True encounter is based on self-transcendence rather than mere self-expression. Specifically, true encounter transcends itself toward the logos. Pseudo-encounter, on the other hand, is based on a "dialogue without logos" (Frankl, 1967). It is only a platform of mutual self-expression. The reason this type of encounter is so widely practiced today is mainly that today people care so much about being cared for. This, in turn, is due to a deficit. In the impersonal climate of industrial society ever more people obviously suffer from a sense of loneliness—the loneliness of "the lonely crowd." Understandably, the intense wish emerges to compensate for this lack of warmth—to compensate for it with closeness. People cry for intimacy. And this cry for intimacy is so urgent that intimacy is sought at any expense, on any level, ironically even on an *impersonal* level, namely, on the level of merely *sensual* intimacy. The cry for intimacy then is converted into the invitation "please touch." And from sensual intimacy it is only one step to sexual promiscuity.

What is needed much more than sexual intimacy is existential privacy. What is greatly needed is to make the best of being lonely, to have "the courage to be" alone. There is also a creative loneliness which makes it possible to turn something negative—the absence of people—into something positive—an opportunity to meditate. By using this opportunity one may make up for the industrial society's all too heavy emphasis on the *vita activa,* and periodically spend some time on the *vita contemplativa.* From this we may see that the real opposite to activity is not passivity but rather receptivity. What is important is a sound balance between the creative and the experiential potentials of meaning fulfillment, and here the justification of "sensitivity training" becomes obvious.

As to those who so much yearn to be cared for, the trouble is that under prevalent conditions they have to pay for it, and it is not hard to imagine how much genuine interest might be shown by those "caretakers" who are not bound by professional ethics and are neither properly trained nor properly supervised. In an age in which hypocrisy in sexual matters is so much abhorred, one should see to it that sexual promiscuity is not labeled sensitivity, or encounter. As compared with those who sell sex under the guise of sex education, nude marathon and so on, one may appreciate the honesty of the average prostitute: she does not pretend that she carries out her business for the benefit of mankind—whose ills, as many an author would like to make us believe, have to be traced back to poor orgasm and treated accordingly. It is true that we often fail to live up to the ideals of our professional ethics; to fail, after all, is part and parcel of the human condition, but if we do fail we will certainly not pride ourselves on our failure. In certain circles, however, this is precisely what happens, ever more frequently. Freud knew all too well what he did when he set up the rule against acting out one's own countertransference. The fact that exceptions to the rule occasionally occur does not justify making the exception into the rule.

Yet the present cult of intimacy is understandable. As Irvin Yalom (1970) pointed out, mobility of the United States population accounts for much of the alienation in people who are used to migrating from one city to another. However, I would say that alienation concerns not only others but also oneself. There is a social alienation, and there is an emotional alienation—alienation from one's own emotions. For too long a time, owing to the puritanism that predominated in Anglo-Saxon countries, people had not only to control but even to suppress their emotions. Something analogous held for the repression of the sex instinct. Since then, to be sure, there has been a swing to the opposite extreme, especially with the popularization, not to say vulgarization, of Freud's teachings. Today we see the consequences of extreme permissiveness: people display an intolerance of instinctual frustration *and* emotional tension; they exhibit "incontinence," one might say, in that they cannot restrain their emotions, they cannot refrain from expressing them and sharing them with others.

It is precisely this end to which the "group" lends itself as a means. Here, however, we have to deal not only with a therapy but simultaneously with a symptom. After all, "incontinence" is a defect on the psychic level as well as the somatic. As to the somatic, just consider those cases of arteriosclerosis in which the patient starts laughing or weeping for reasons that are not proportionate, and then cannot stop. This is paralleled by another symptom equally indicating impairment of the brain's function, namely, the absence of a sense of personal distance, as observed in severe epileptic disorders: the patient immediately fraternizes with everybody—he cannot stop informing you about his private life or inquiring about your private life.

To sum up, the encounter group movement and sensitivity training boil down to reactions to social and emotional alienation, respectively. Yet the reaction to a problem must not be confused with a solution to the problem. Even if a "reaction" turns out to be curative, the cure is symptomatic, a palliative. Worse, such a cure may well reinforce the disease. As to the issue at hand, the emotions, they cannot be brought about intentionally to begin with. They elude "hyperintention," as I am used to calling it. Nowhere is this more conspicuous than with regard to happiness: happiness must ensue and cannot be pursued. Happiness must happen, and we must let it happen. Conversely, the more we aim at it, the more we miss our aim. An advanced student of mine who had undertaken independent research on encounter groups reported what had happened to him when he joined one: "I was asked by many persons to be their friend. I did not feel sincere in embracing them and telling them that I loved them and would be their friend, but I did so anyway. I forced myself to be emotional—but to no avail: the harder I tried the more difficult it was."

We have to face the fact that there are certain activities that cannot be demanded, commanded, or ordered. The reason lies in the fact that they cannot be established at will: I cannot "will" to believe; I cannot "will" to hope; I cannot "will" to love; and least of all can I "will" to will. Attempts to do so reflect an entirely manipulative approach to human phenomena such as faith, hope, love and will. This manipulative approach, in turn, is due to an inappropriate objectification and reification of the phenomena in question. In order to understand this better, let us consider what I would say is the main characteristic of any subject, namely, the fact that a subject—by virtue of his self-transcendence, or the intentionality of his cognitive acts—is always related to objects of his own, i.e., the "intentional referents" to which his cognitive acts reach out. To the extent that a subject is made into a mere thing ("reification") and, thus, himself turned into an object ("objectification"), to the same extent his own proper objects necessarily must disappear, so that eventually his subject quality is lost altogether. This holds not only for a human being but for any human phenomenon: the more we reflect on it, the more we lose sight of its own "intentional referent."

Relaxation too eludes any attempt to "manufacture" it. This was fully taken into account by J. H. Schultz, who systematized relaxation exercises. How wise was he when he directed his patients, during these exercises, to imagine their arms becoming heavy; this automatically induced relaxation. If he had *ordered* these patients to relax, their tenseness would have increased, because they would have intensely and intentionally *striven* for relaxation. It is not different with the treatment of inferiority feelings: the patient will never succeed in overcoming them by way of a direct attempt. If he is to get rid of inferiority feelings he has to do so, so to speak, on a detour, for instance, by going places *despite* inferiority feelings, or by doing his job in spite of them. As long as he centers attention on the inferiority feelings within himself, and "fights" them, he continues suffering from them; however, as soon as he focuses attention on something outside himself, say, a task, they are doomed to atrophy.

Paying too much attention to something is what I am used to calling "hyper-reflection." This parallels hyper-intention insofar as both may result in neuroses. And, as a matter of fact, both may be reinforced and enhanced by the "group." In this setting, the patient is invited carefully to observe and watch himself; what is even more important, he is encouraged by the individual members endlessly to discuss with them whatever he furnishes from within himself. "Hyper-discussion" might be an apt term for what goes on in such situations. And hyper-discussion becomes more and more a substitute for the meaning of life which today is so often missing, and missed by those among our patients who are caught in an "existential vacuum" (Frankl, 1955), a feeling of emptiness and meaninglessness. In this vacuum, neuroses hypertrophy. Conversely, once the existential vacuum is filled up, they often atrophy.

One cannot but fully agree with what Charlotte Bühler (1970) says: "In spite of much confusion and concern with negative side-effects, certain essential benefits of the encounter-group movement seem clear." And among the main benefits, she lists "the spirit of cooperation and mutual helpfulness." Indeed, a properly conceived encounter group can surely provide a context of mutual assistance in which to discuss life's meaning. The properly conceived encounter group not only indulges in the self-expression of the individual members but also promotes their self-transcendence. Or, as Robert M. Holmes (1970) says, "group logotherapy could pay large dividends." What Holmes envisions are "possibilities of implementing the logotherapeutic philosophy in concrete group situations." And he concludes his paper as follows: "Who could predict the results of such a group—called to discuss their own failures, their own 'existential vacuum'? What personal discoveries might be made in the discipline of telling one's own story from the standpoint of one's search for meaning in the unavoidable facts of his life?"

REFERENCES

Bühler, Ch. (1970), Group psychotherapy as related to problems of our time, *Interpersonal Development,* 1, 3–5.

Bühler, Ch., and M. Allen (1972), "Introduction into Humanistic Psychology," Belmont: Brooks/Cole.

Frankl, V. E. (1955), "The Doctor and the Soul: From Psychotherapy to Logotherapy," Bantam Books, New York.

Frankl, V. E. (1962), "Man's Search for Meaning: An Introduction to Logotherapy," Beacon Press, Boston.

Frankl, V. E. (1967), "Psychotherapy and Existentialism: Selected Papers on Logotherapy," Simon and Schuster, New York.

Holmes, R. M. (1970), Alcoholics anonymous as group logotherapy. *Pastoral Psych.,* 21, 30–36.

Spiegelberg, H. (1972), "Phenomenology in Psychology and Psychiatry," Northwestern University Press, New York.

Yalom, I. D. (1970), "The Theory and Practice of Group Psychotherapy," Basic Books, New York.

The Dehumanization of Sex*

ONE CANNOT SPEAK OF HUMAN SEX WITHOUT SPEAK-
ing of love. When speaking of love, however, we
should remember that it is a specifically human phenomenon. And we must see to it that it is preserved in
its humanness, rather than treated in a reductionistic
way.

What precisely is reductionism? I would define it as
a pseudo-scientific procedure that takes human phenomena and either reduces them to or deduces them
from subhuman phenomena. Love, for example,
would be interpreted as the sublimation of sexual
drives and instincts which man shares with the other
animals. Such an interpretation can only block a true
understanding of the human phenomenon.

Love is really one aspect of a more encompassing
human phenomenon which I have come to call self-
transcendence (Frankl, 1963). Man is not, as the predominant motivation theories would like us to believe,

---

* Revised and enlarged version of the paper "Love and Society,"
which was translated into Japanese and published in the volume:
Pathology of Modern Men, edited by Sadayo Ishikawa. Tokyo:
Seishin Shobo, 1974.

basically concerned with gratifying his needs and satisfying his drives and instincts, and thereby maintaining, or restoring, homeostasis, i.e., the inner equilibrium. Rather, man is—by virtue of the self-transcendent quality of the human reality—basically concerned with reaching out beyond himself, be it toward a meaning to fulfill, or toward another human being lovingly to encounter.

Loving encounter, however, definitely precludes regarding or using another human being as a mere means to an end—as a tool for reducing the tensions created by libidinal, or aggressive, drives and instincts. This would amount to masturbation, and in fact that is how many of our sexually neurotic patients speak of the way they treat their partners: in fact they often say they "masturbate on their partners." Such an attitude toward a partner is a specifically neurotic distortion of human sex.

Human sex is always more than mere sex, and it is more than sex to the extent that it serves as the physical expression of something metasexual, is the physical expression of love. Only to the extent that sex carries out this function is it a really rewarding experience. Maslow (1964) was justified in pointing out that "the people who can't love don't get the same kind of thrill out of sex as the people who can love" (p.105). According to 20,000 readers of an American psychological magazine who answered a pertinent questionnaire, the factor that is most enhancing to potency and orgasm is romanticism—that is to say, something that comes close to love.

Still, it is not quite accurate to say that human sex is more than mere sex. As Irenaeus Eibl-Eibesfeldt

(1970) has evidenced, in some vertebrates sexual behavior also serves group cohesion, and this is particularly the case with primates that live in groups. Thus, in certain apes sexual intercourse sometimes exclusively serves a social purpose; in humans, Eibl-Eibesfeldt states, there is no doubt that sexual intercourse is conducive not only to the propagation of the species but also the monogamous relation between the partners.

While love is a human phenomenon by its very nature, sex becomes human only as the result of a developmental process, the product of progressive maturation (Frankl, 1955). Let us start with Sigmund Freud's differentiation between the goal of drives and instincts, and their object: the goal of sex is the reduction of sexual tensions, whereas the object of sex is the sexual partner. As I see it, this holds only for neurotic sexuality: only a neurotic individual is out first and foremost to get rid of his sperma, be it by masturbation or by using the partner as just another means to the same end. To the mature person the partner is no "object" at all; the mature person, rather, sees in the partner another subject, another human being, seeing him in his very humanness; and if he really loves him, he even sees in the partner another person, which means that he sees in him his uniqueness. This uniqueness constitutes the personhood of a human being, and it is only love that enables one person to seize hold of another in this way.

Grasping the uniqueness of a loved one understandably results in a monogamous partnership. The partner is no longer interchangeable. Conversely, if one is not able to love, he winds up with promiscuity.* Indulging in promiscuity implies ignoring the partner's uniqueness and this in turn precludes a love relationship. Since only that sex which is embedded in love can be really rewarding and satisfactory, the quality of the sexual life of such an individual is poor. Small wonder, then, that he tries to compensate for this lack of quality with quantity. This, in turn, requires an ever increased and intensified stimulation, as is provided, for one, by pornography.

From this it should be clear we are in no way justified in glorifying such mass phenomena as promiscuity and pornography or in considering them progressive. They are regressive; they are symptoms of a retardation in one's sexual maturation.

But we should not forget either that the myth of sex just for fun's sake as something progressive is promoted by people who know it is good business. What intrigues me is the fact that the young generation not only buys the myth but is blind to the hypocrisy behind it. In an age when hypocrisy in sexual matters is so frowned upon, it is strange that the hypocrisy of those who promulgate a certain freedom from censorship remains unnoticed. Is it so hard to recognize that their real concern is unlimited freedom to make money?

There can be no successful business unless there is a substantial demand that the business meets. In our present culture we are witnessing what one might call an inflation of sex. This is understandable only against

_____
* As masturbation means being content with tension reduction as a goal, so promiscuity means being content with the partner as an object. In neither case is the human potential of sex actualized.

the more comprehensive background of the existential vacuum and the fact that man, no longer told by drives and instincts what he must do or by traditions and values what he should do, now often no longer knows what he wishes to do.

In the existential vacuum resulting from this state of affairs, the sexual libido hypertrophies, and it is this hypertrophy that brings about the inflation of sex. Like any other kind of inflation—e.g., that on the monetary market—sexual inflation is associated with a devaluation: sex is devaluated inasmuch as it is dehumanized. Thus, we observe a trend to living a sexual life that is not integrated into one's personal life, but rather is lived out for the sake of pleasure. Such a depersonalization of sex is a symptom of existential frustration: the frustration of man's search for meaning.

So much for causes; but what about the effects? The more one's search for meaning is frustrated, the more intensively he devotes himself to what since the American Declaration of Independence has been termed the "pursuit of happiness." When this pursuit originates in a frustrated search for meaning it is aimed at intoxication and stupefaction. In the final analysis it is self-defeating, for happiness can arise only as a result of living out one's self-transcendence, one's dedication to a cause to be served or a person to be loved.

Nowhere is this more evident than in regard to sexual happiness. The more we make it an aim, the more we miss it. The more concerned a male patient is with his potency, the more likely he is to become impotent; the more a female patient tries to demonstrate to herself that she is capable of fully experiencing orgasm, the more liable she is to be caught in frigidity. Most of the cases of sexual neurosis I have encountered in my many decades of psychiatric practice can easily be traced back to this state of affairs.

As I have elaborated elsewhere (Frankl, 1952, 1955; also see "Paradoxical Intention and Dereflection" in this book), sexual neurotics usually ascribe what may be called a demand quality to sexual achievement. Accordingly, attempts to cure such cases have to start with removing this quality. I have developed a technique by which such a treatment can be implemented, and published it in English for the first time in the *International Journal of Sexology* (Frankl, 1952). All I want to point out here, however, is the fact that our present culture, due to the motivation outlined above, idolizes sexual achievement and further adds to the demand quality experienced by the sexually neurotic individual, thus further contributing to his neurosis.

The Pill too, by allowing the female partner to be more demanding and spontaneous, encourages the male partners to experience sexual intercourse as something that is demanded of them. American authors even blame the woman's liberation movement for having freed women of old taboos and inhibitions to the extent that even college girls are demanding sexual satisfaction—demanding it from college boys. The result has been a new set of problems variously called "college impotence," or "the new impotence" (Ginsberg *et al.*, 1972).*

---

* Women have learned about orgasm," says Nyles A. Freedman, director of Sexual Health Centers of New England, Inc. "There is a destructive emphasis on performance which can create anxiety and fear of functioning. Sexual impotence is increasing, at least partly

We observe something analogous on the subhuman level. There is a species of fish whose females habitually swim "coquettishly" away from the males who seek to mate. However, Konrad Lorenz succeeded in training a female to do the very opposite—to forcefully approach the male. The latter's reaction? Just what we would have expected of a college boy: a complete incapacity to carry out sexual intercourse!

As to the Pill, we have discussed only a side effect, a negative effect. Looking at its positive side, we have to acknowledge that it is rendering an inestimable service. If it is true that it is love that makes sex human, it is the Pill that frees sex from its automatic connection with procreation and thus allows it to become, and remain, a pure expression of love. Human sex, as we have said, must never be made into a mere tool in the service of the pleasure principle. As we now see, however, neither should it be a mere means to an end that is dictated by the procreation instinct. The Pill has emancipated sex from such tyranny and has thereby made it possible to actualize its real potential.

Victorian sexual taboos and inhibitions are on the wane, and freedom in sexual matters has been gained. What we must not forget is that freedom threatens to degenerate into mere license and arbitrariness unless it is lived in terms of responsibleness.

---

due to what males expect females to expect." And Dena K. Whitebook of the American Institute of Family Relations puts the blame more squarely on the unreasonable demands of women. (*Newsweek*, January 16, 1978.)

REFERENCES

Irenaeus Eibl-Eibesfeldt, *Frankfurter Allgemeine Zeitung* (February 28, 1970).

Frankl, Viktor E., "The Pleasure Principle and Sexual Neurosis." *The International Journal of Sexology,* 5, 1952, 128.

———, *The Doctor and the Soul.* New York, Knopf, 1955.

———, *Man's Search for Meaning.* New York, Washington Square Press, 1963.

George L. Ginsberg, William A. Frosch and Theodor Shapiro, "The New Impotence." *Arch. Gen. Psychiat.,* 26, 1972, 218.

Abraham H. Maslow, *Religions, Values, and Peak-Experiences.* Columbus, Ohio State University Press, 1964.

Symptom or Therapy?
A Psychiatrist Looks
at Modern Literature*

WHEN I WAS INVITED TO ADDRESS THIS MEETING I
first felt somewhat reluctant. There are so many repre-
sentatives of modern literature dabbling in the field of
psychiatry—to be sure, a rather obsolete sort of psychiatry—I hate to become a psychiatrist dabbling in
the field of modern literature. What is more important,
it does not go without question that psychiatry has
anything to say on the subject of modern literature. It
simply is not true that psychiatry has the answers.
Even today we psychiatrists don't know, for example,
what is the real cause of schizophrenia. Even less do
we know how to cure it. As I often say, we are neither
omniscient nor omnipotent; the only divine attribute
you may ascribe to us is omnipresence—you find us on
every panel and on each symposium, even at your
meeting . . .

---

* Lecture delivered as guest of honor at the meeting of International
P.E.N. held in the Hilton Hotel in Vienna, November 18, 1975.

I think we should *stop divinizing psychiatry—and start humanizing it*. To begin with, we must learn to differentiate between what is human in man and what is pathological in him—in other words, between what is a mental or emotional disease on the one hand, and on the other, what is, for instance, existential despair, despair over the apparent meaninglessness of human existence—indeed, a favorite topic of modern literature, isn't it? Sigmund Freud, it is true, once wrote that "The moment one inquires about the sense or value of life, one is sick"; but I rather think that one thereby manifests one's humanness. It is a human achievement to quest for a meaning to life, and even to question whether such a meaning is available at all.

Even if in a given case we conclude that an author is really sick, not merely neurotic but psychotic, does this necessarily speak against the truth or the worth of his work? I don't think so. *Two times two equals four remains true even if a schizophrenic individual makes the statement*. Likewise, I believe that it does not detract from Hoelderlin's poetry or the truth of Nietzsche's philosophy that the former was suffering from a schizophrenia and the latter from general paresis. I am sure that Hoelderlin and Nietzsche will still be read and their names revered when the names of those psychiatrists who have turned out volumes on the psychoses of the two "cases" are long forgotten.

The presence of pathology does not speak against a writer's work; yet neither does it speak in favor of it. No psychotic writer has ever created an important work because of his psychosis, but only in spite of it. *Illness per se is never creative.*

* * *

In recent times it has become a fad to look at modern literature from the psychiatric viewpoint, and in particular to see it as the product of unconscious psychodynamics. Consequently, so-called depth psychology has come to see its principal assignment in terms of unmasking the hidden motivation that underlies literary production. To show you what happens when one puts a writer on what I like to call the "procrustean couch," let me quote a review, published in the *Journal of Existentialism*, of two volumes that a famous Freudian devoted to Goethe: "In the 1538 pages, the author portrays to us a genius with the earmarks of a manic-depressive, paranoid, and epileptoid disorder, of homosexuality, incest, voyeurism, exhibitionism, fetishism, impotence, narcissism, obsessive-compulsive neurosis, hysteria, megalomania, etc. The author seems to focus exclusively upon the instinctual dynamic forces that underlie the artistic product. We are led to believe that Goethe's work is but the result of pregenital fixations. His struggle does not really aim for an ideal, for beauty, for values, but for the overcoming of an embarrassing problem of premature ejaculation."*

I think that unmasking has to stop once the unmasking psychologist is confronted with what is genuine. If he does not stop there, what he unmasks then is his own unconscious motivation, namely, to belittle the hidden greatness of man.

One wonders why the business of unmasking and debunking is so attractive to the reader. It seems to be a relief to hear that Goethe too was nothing but a

---

* *Journal of Existentialism,* 5, 1964, p. 229.

neurotic—to say the least—like you and me and every other neurotic (and let him who is without neurotic flaws be the first to cast a stone at us). In a way, it is also good to hear that man is nothing but a "naked ape"; the playground of id, ego and superego; the pawn and plaything of drives and instincts; the product of conditioning and learning processes; the victim of socioeconomic circumstances, hang-ups and complexes.

As Brian Goodwin once so aptly observed, "It is good for people to face that they are nothing but this or that, much as it is sometimes believed that good medicine must have a nasty taste."* It seems to me, too, that at least some of the people to whom debunking is so appealing take a masochistic pleasure in the *nothing-but-ness* that is preached by reductionism.

To come back to the debunking of modern literature, whether the alleged roots of literary production are abnormal or normal, whether they are unconscious or conscious, the fact remains that writing is more often than not regarded as an act of self-expression. However, it is my contention that writing follows speaking, and speaking in turn follows thinking; and there is no thinking without something that is thought of, and meant. The same holds for writing and speaking inasmuch as they too are always related to a meaning they have to convey. Unless it has such a message, language is not really language. It simply is not true that

---

* "Science and Alchemy," in *The Rules of the Game: Cross-disciplinary Essays on Models in Scholarly Thought*. Ed. by Teodor Shanin. London: Tavistock Publications, 1972, p. 375.

"the medium is the message"; rather, I think that it is *only the message* that *makes the medium into a real medium.*

Language is more than mere self-expression.* Language is always pointing to something beyond itself. In other words, it is always self-transcendent—as is human existence at large. Being human is always directed to something, or someone, other than itself, to a meaning to fulfill or another human being to encounter. Like the healthy eye, which does not see itself, man, too, functions best when he is overlooking and forgetting himself, by giving himself. Forgetting himself makes for *sensitivity,* and giving himself, for *creativity.*

By virtue of the self-transcendence of human existence man is a being in search of meaning. He is dominated by a will to meaning. Today, however, the will to meaning is frustrated. Ever more patients turn to us psychiatrists complaining of feelings of meaninglessness and emptiness, of *a sense of futility and absurdity.* They are victims of the mass neurosis of today.

This feeling of meaninglessness may have something to do with the general theme of your meeting. Three decades of relative peace have enabled man to think beyond the struggle for survival. Now we ask what is the ultimate meaning beyond survival—if there is any at all? In the words of Ernst Bloch, "Today, men have

---

* With the sole exception of schizophrenic language. Years ago, I showed through experimentation that the language of schizophrenics is no longer directed to an object, but merely expresses the mood of the subject.

been granted those concerns which they formerly had been confronted with only on their deathbeds."

Such worldwide phenomena as violence and drug addiction, as well as the staggering suicide rates, particularly among academic youth, are some of its symptoms; but also part of modern literature is a symptom. As long as modern literature confines itself to, and contents itself with, self-expression—not to say self-exhibition—it reflects its authors' sense of futility and absurdity. What is more important, it also creates absurdity. This is understandable in light of the fact that meaning must be discovered, it cannot be invented. Sense cannot be created, but what may well be created is nonsense.

Small wonder that a writer who is caught in the feeling of meaninglessness would be tempted to fill the emptiness with nonsense and absurdity.

However, there is another option. Modern literature need not remain just another symptom of the mass neurosis of today. It can as well contribute to the therapy. Writers who themselves have gone through the hell of despair over the apparent meaninglessness of life can offer their suffering as a sacrifice on the altar of humankind. Their self-disclosure can help the reader who is plagued by the same condition, help him in overcoming it.

The least service the writer could render the reader would be to evoke a sense of *solidarity*. In this case, the symptom would be the therapy. However, if modern literature is to carry out this therapeutic assignment—in other words, if it is to actualize its *therapeutic potential*—it has to refrain from turning nihilism into cynicism. As justified as the writer might be in sharing his own sense of futility with the reader, it is irresponsible cynically to preach the absurdity of existence. If the writer is not capable of *immunizing the reader against despair,* he should at least refrain from *inoculating him with despair.*

Tomorrow I shall have the honor of giving the opening address at the Austria Book Fair. The title I have selected is "The Book as Therapy." In other words, I shall be speaking on *healing through reading.* I shall tell my audience of cases in which a book has changed the life of the reader, and of other cases in which a book has saved his life by preventing him from committing suicide. I shall include cases in which a book has helped people on their deathbed and people in prison. I shall include the case Aaron Mitchell, the last victim of the gas chamber at San Quentin prison near San Francisco. I had gone to address the prisoners at the request of the prison's director. When I finished, one stood up and asked if I would say a few words to Aaron Mitchell, who was to be executed in a few days. It was a challenge I had to accept, so I told Mr. Mitchell about my own experience in the Nazi concentration camps, when I too had lived in the shadow of a gas chamber. Even then, I told him, I did not give up my conviction of the unconditional meaningfulness of life, because either life has a meaning—and then it must retain its meaning even if it is briefly lived—or life has no meaning, in which case adding more years and perpetuating this meaningless job could not be of any meaning either. "And, believe me," I said, "even a life that has been meaningless all along, that is, a life that has been wasted, may—even in the last moment—still be bestowed with meaning by the very way in which we tackle this situation." To illustrate, I told him the story that is laid down in Leo Tolstoy's novel *The Death of Ivan Ilyich*—as you remember, the tale of a man about sixty years old who suddenly learns that he is to die in a couple of days. But by the insight he gains, not only in facing death but also in confronting the fact that he has wasted his life, that his life has been virtually meaningless—by this insight he rises above himself, he grows beyond himself and thereby finally becomes capable, retroactively, of flooding his life with infinite meaning.

Shortly before his execution, Aaron Mitchell gave an interview written up in the San Francisco *Chronicle* in which he left no doubt that Tolstoy's message had reached him.

From this you may gather how much also the man in the street may benefit from an author, even in an extreme life situation, not to say a death situation. You may see as well how far-reaching the author's social responsibility is. It is true, the author should be granted the freedom of opinion and its expression; but freedom is not the last word, it is not the whole story. Freedom threatens to degenerate into arbitrariness unless it is balanced by responsibleness.

Sports—
The Asceticism of Today*

I WOULD LIKE TO TALK ABOUT SPORTS IN THE WIDEST sense—that is to say, about *sports as a human phenomenon*. This implies that I am going to talk about the authentic phenomenon rather than its *degeneration* into Olympic *chauvinism* or its *misuse* through *commercialism*. However, access to the authentic phenomenon called sports is blocked as long as its analysis still adheres to that concept of man which still prevails in current motivation theories. According to these theories man is a being who has certain needs and is out to satisfy them, in the final analysis, only to the end of "tension reduction"—i.e., in order to maintain or restore an inner equilibrium which is called "homeostasis." Homeostasis is a concept borrowed from biology, but which has since been shown to be untenable there. Ludwig von Bertalanffy evidenced that primordial biological phenomena such as growth and reproduction cannot be explained in terms of the

---

* Paper read at the scientific congress sponsored by the Olympic Games, Munich, 1972.

homeostasis principle, and Kurt Goldstein even proved that only a brain that is functioning pathologically is characterized by the attempt to avoid tensions unconditionally. I myself think that man is never primarily concerned with any such inner condition but rather always with something, or someone, out in the world, be it a cause to serve or a partner to love (which means that the partner is not regarded just as a means to the end of need satisfaction). In other words, human existence—at least as long as it is not neurotically distorted—is always pointing and related to something other than itself. I have termed this constitutive characteristic "the self-transcendence of human existence." Self-actualization is possible only as a by-product of self-transcendence.*

In contrast to the homeostasis hypothesis, I would like to propound the following four theses: (1) Man not only does not primarily care for tension reduction—he even *needs tensions*. (2) Therefore, he is *in search of tensions*. (3) Today, however, he does not find enough tension. (4) That is why he sometimes creates tensions.

(1) It goes without saying that man should not be subjected to too much tension. What he needs is rather a moderate amount, a sound amount, a sound dosage, of tension.† Not only too-great demands, but also the

---

* One should not confuse this with any transcendental matters in the religious sense. "Self-transcendence" refers only to the fact that the more a human being forgets himself and gives himself, the more human he is.

† Human existence is characterized not only by its self-trancendence but also by its capacity of self-detachment. It should be observed also that a certain distance between the real state of affairs

contrary, the lack of challenges, may cause disease. In this sense, Werner Schulte once cited the discharge of tensions as a typical origin of nervous breakdowns. Even Selye, the father of the stress concept, recently admitted that "stress is the salt of life." I myself would go one step further and claim that man needs a specific tension, namely, the kind of tension that is established between a human being, on the one hand, and, on the other hand, a meaning he has to fulfill. In fact, if an individual is not challenged by any tasks to complete, and thus is *spared* the specific tension aroused by such tasks, a certain type of neurosis—noögenic neurosis—may ensue.

(2) Thus it emerges that man is not just in search of tensions per se, but in particular, in search of tasks whose completion might add meaning to his existence. Man is basically motivated by what I call the "will to meaning," as empirical research in recent years has confirmed.

(3) Today, however, many people are no longer able to find such a meaning and purpose. In contrast to the findings of Sigmund Freud, man is no longer sexually frustrated, in the first place, but rather "existentially frustrated." And in contrast to the findings of Alfred Adler, his main complaint is no longer a feeling of inferiority but rather a feeling of futility, a feeling of meaninglessness and emptiness, which I have termed the "existential vacuum." Its main symptom is boredom! In the last century Arthur Schopenhauer said

---

and the ideal is intrinsic to our being human; and empirical research has shown that too little tension between the ego and the ego ideal is as detrimental to mental health as too much tension.

that mankind appeared to be doomed eternally to vacillate between the two extremes of want and boredom;* today we have arrived at the latter extreme. Affluent society has given vast segments of population the means, but people cannot see an end, a meaning to live for. In addition, we are living in a leisure society; ever more people have ever more time to spend, but nothing meaningful on which to spend it. All this adds up to the obvious conclusion that to the degree that man is spared want and tension he loses the capacity to endure them. Most importantly, he becomes incapable of renunciation. But Hoelderlin was right when he said that where danger lurks, there rescue is near. As affluent society offers too little tension, man starts creating tensions.

(4) He artificially creates the tension that he has been spared by affluent society! He provides himself with tensions by deliberately placing demands on himself—by voluntarily exposing himself to stress situations, if only temporarily. As I see it, this is precisely the function carried out by sports! Sports allow man to build up situations of emergency. What he then demands of himself is unnecessary achievement—and unnecessary sacrifice. In the midst of a sea of affluence, islands of asceticism emerge! In fact, I regard sports as the modern, the secular, form of asceticism.

What did I mean by unnecessary accomplishment? We are living in an age when man need not walk—he may drive his car. He does not need to climb stairs—

---

* I think that there are also periods of repressive styles of education over against periods of a permissive style. At present extreme permissiveness seems to be on the wane.

he may take the elevator. So, in this very situation, he suddenly takes up scaling mountains! For "the naked ape" there is no longer any need to climb trees, so he deliberately and voluntarily takes up climbing mountains and scaling steep cliffs! Although there is no climbing at the Olympic Games, I hope you will make allowance for my focusing for a while on the sport of rock climbing.

I have said that in rock climbing man artificially creates necessities he has been spared by evolution. However, this interpretation is restricted to rock climbing up to the third degree of difficulty—no ape has ever been able to perform any climbing beyond the third degree. Even the famous apes that climb around the cliffs of Gibraltar would not be able to cope with the difficulties met last week by some rock climbers from the Tyrol and Bavaria when they were the first to master the Sugar Hat in Rio de Janeiro. But let us remember the technical definition of the sixth degree of difficulty in rock climbing—it reads: *Close to the ultimate limits of human possibilities!* And that is it: the so-called "extreme" rock climber goes beyond (artificial) *necessities;* he is interested in *possibilities*— he wonders where the ultimate limits of human possibilities lie! And he wishes to find out. But the limits turn out to be nowhere, like the horizon, because man pushes them ever farther with each step he takes toward them.

There are other interpretations of sports which in no way do justice to the humanness of the phenomenon. These not only bypass the function of secular asceticism, but also are based on an old-fashioned, outdated motivation theory that depicts man as a being to whom the world ultimately serves as a mere means to gratify drives and instincts, including aggressive impulses, in order to get rid of the inner tensions created by them. However, contrary to this closed-system concept, man is a being who is reaching out for meanings to fulfill and other human beings to encounter, and certainly these are more to him than just a means to the end of living out his aggressive and sexual drives and instincts.

However, regarding the alternative to living them out—that is, the possibility of sublimating them—Carolyn Wood Sherif has warned us against harboring an illusion that is characteristic of the closed-system concepts of man, namely, the illusion that aggression can be drained by channeling it into harmless activities, such as sports. On the contrary, "there is a substantial body of research evidence that the successful execution of aggressive actions, far from reducing subsequent aggression, is the best way to increase the frequency of aggressive responses (such studies have included both animal and human behavior)."

One may find that not only sexual libido thrives in an existential vacuum, but also aggressive "destrudo." Robert Jay Lifton seems to agree with me when he states that "men are most apt to kill when they feel overcome by meaninglessness,"* and statistical evidence is favorable to this hypothesis.

Now let us ask how my theory of sports may be applied to the practice of sports. I said that man is curious to locate the limits of his possibilities, but by approaching them, he pushes them ever farther, like

* *History and Human Survival* (New York: Random House, 1969).

the horizon. From this it follows that in any competition in sports man is really *competing with himself*. He is *his own rival*. At least he should be. This is no moral prescription but a factual statement, because the more someone is out to compete with others and defeat them, the less he is able to actualize his potential. Contrariwise, the more he concentrates on just giving his best, without caring too much for his success and triumph over the others, the sooner and more easily his efforts will be crowned by success. There are things that elude direct intention; they can be obtained only as the side effects of intending something else. When they are made an aim, the aim is missed. Sexual happiness is an example: one cannot achieve it by trying.

Something analogous holds for sports. Try to give your best and you are likely to wind up as a winner; conversely, try to win and you are liable to lose. You then become tense rather than remaining relaxed. To put it in a lighter vein, you should not try to demonstrate that "you are the greatest" but rather try to find out "who is greater—you or you," to quote from a famous comedy of Old Vienna. In fact, Ilona Gusenbauer (who until the 1972 Olympic Games in Munich held the world record in high jumping) recently said in an interview, "I must not tell myself that defeating the others is a must." To cite another example, the Austrian national soccer team was behind the Hungarians 0:2 at halftime. The Austrians were "depressed, discouraged and pessimistic," to quote their coach, but they resumed the match in high spirits after the pause. What had happened? Herr Stastny, the coach, had told them that they still had a chance, but that he would not blame them for a defeat—provided that they now really gave their best. The outcome was admirable— 2:2.

The optimal motivation in sports—to maximize the results—requires that one compete with oneself rather than with others. Such an attitude is antagonistic to "hyperintention," by which term logotherapy denotes the neurotic habit of making something the target of both intention and attention. Paradoxical intention is a logotherapeutic technique devised to counteract hyperintention. It has been successfully used in the treatment of neuroses, and Robert L. Korzep, the coach of an American baseball team, attests that it is also applicable in sports. At the Logotherapy Institute of the U.S. International University at San Diego, California, he summarized his pertinent experience in the following statement: "I am an athletic coach and very much interested in mental attitude and the effects it may have on winning or losing in team sports. It is my contention that logotherapy may be utilized or be applicable to situations that arise in athletics—i.e., pressure situations, pregame anxiety, fighting slumps, lack of confidence, sacrifice and dedication, and problem athletes. In my coaching experiences, I can now look back and see related incidents in sports that involved both individual and group behavior that might have been remedied with . . . logotherapeutic technique. I am particularly enthusiastic about the possibilities the logotherapeutic concept of paradoxical intention presents for athletics."

Warren Jeffrey Byers, who has been a swimming coach for a number of years, also has reported "some experiences about the application of logotherapy to competitive swimming," as follows: "Logotherapy has application to the actual mechanics of coaching. Every coach knows that tenseness is the enemy of superior performance. The primary cause of tenseness during the swimming event is *being overly concerned with victory,* or *hyperintending* success. The athlete may be concerned with beating the swimmer in the next lane. The minute the athlete hyperintends success he will turn in an inferior performance. If the athlete hyperintends, he may forego his sense of pace for that of his opponent. The swimmer will look over at his opponent to see how things are progressing. When coaching a student with this problem I stress the importance of swimming his own race. I have also used a form of *paradoxical intention.* There is another negative consequence of hyperintention. I have known athletes who became extremely nervous and anxious before swimming meets. They would lose sleep especially the night before the race. The task is to calm them down. I use a form of dereflection. I want the athlete to focus away from winning the race and toward swimming his own race. The athlete will swim best if he attempts to *be his own best rival.* These are a few ways logotherapy applies to the world of competitive swimming and my activities as a coach. I feel that logotherapy can be a powerful coaching tool. Unfortunately not many coaches have been exposed to the techniques of logotherapy. There is no doubt that when the word gets out to more coaches through the swimming journals the use of logotherapy in swimming will be widespread."

Now let us give a hearing to an athlete who once was European champion: "I was unbeaten for seven years.

Later I was on the national team. Now I had pressure on me. *I had to win,* the whole nation expected that. The time before every race was awful." Hyperintention developed at the expense of comradeship: "These guys"—his comrades—"are always the best friends except right before the race, when they hate each other."

Contrast with that what E. Kim Adams, a former student of mine and a champion in sport parachuting, has to say about another star athlete: *"The real athlete competes only against himself.* The present absolute world champion in sport parachuting is Clay Schoelpple, a fellow I grew up with. In analyzing why the U.S.A. and not the U.S.S.R. won the last meet, he said simply that they came to win. Clay competes only against himself." And it was he who won.

POSTSCRIPT: Dr. Terry Orlick is a professor in the psychology of sport at the University of Ottawa. He recommends "something Frankl refers to as 'paradoxical intention.' Instead of trying to get rid of the anxiety, you try to hang on to it, and it goes away by itself. If you get so anxious that you sweat off two pounds before an important event begins, try to sweat off four pounds. Some athletes find this approach very effective. I can recall two recent cases where anxiety-prone athletes felt that it helped performances in competitions which were very important to them. One of the athletes began to get very anxious before his tournament. He asked himself, 'What am I anxious about?' Then he said to himself, 'I'll show them how anxious I can be. As I tried to heighten my anxiety it went away.' The other athlete was so anxious before competing in a world title event that she was almost sick to her stomach. Instead of trying to relax away the tension, she tried to experience it to the fullest. She said to herself, 'I'm so anxious I'm going to be sick.' Then 'thought about how ridiculous it was, laughed, and it went away.' " (*In Pursuit of Excellence*, Ottawa, Coaching Association of Canada, 1980, pp. 124–125.)

Temporality and Mortality:
An Ontological Essay*

FACE TO FACE WITH LIFE'S TRANSITORINESS WE MAY say that the future does not yet exist; the past does not exist any more; and the only thing that really exists is the present. Or we may say that the future is nothing; the past too is nothing; and man is a being coming out of nothingness; "thrown" into being; and threatened by nothingness. How, then, in view of the essential transitoriness of human existence, can man find meaning in life?

Existential philosophy asserts that he can. What this philosophy calls "tragic heroism" is the possibility of saying yes to life in spite of its transitoriness. Existentialism places the emphasis on the present—however transitory the present might be.

The opposite may be said of quietism which, in the tradition of Plato and St. Augustine, holds that eter-

---

* Based on a paper titled *"Der seelisch kranke Mensch vor der Frage nach dem Sinn des Daseins"* ("Neurosis and the Quest for Meaning"), which I read at the University of Innsbruck in the Tyrol on February 19, 1947.

nity rather than the present is the true reality. To be sure, what is meant by eternity is a simultaneous world that encompasses present, past and future. In other words, what is denied is neither the reality of the past nor that of the future but rather the reality of time as such. Eternity is seen as a four-dimensional world—permanent, rigid and predetermined. According to quietism, time is imaginary, and the past, the present and the future are mere illusions of our consciousness. Everything exists simultaneously. Events do not follow each other in a temporal sequence, but what appears to be a temporal sequence is only a self-deception caused by our consciousness gliding along the "events," i.e., the individual aspects of the unchanging reality, which do not follow each other but really coexist.

It is understandable that quietism by necessity leads to fatalism: if everything already "is," nothing can be changed and there is no point in action. This fatalism, born out of a belief in an unchangeable being, has its counterpart in the pessimism of existentialism, which is the consequence of the belief that everything is unstable and changing.

Logotherapy takes a middle position between quietism and existentialism, and this can best be elucidated by the analogy of the hourglass, the ancient symbol of time. The upper part of the hourglass would represent the future—that which is still to come, like the sand in the upper part that will pass through the narrow opening representing the present; and the lower part of the hourglass would represent the past—the sand that already has passed the narrow passage. Existentialism then sees only the narrow passage of the present while disregarding the upper and the lower parts, the future and the past. Quietism, on the other hand, sees the hourglass in its totality but considers the sand as an inert mass that does not "flow" but simply "is."

Logotherapy would claim that, while it is true that the future really "is not," the past is the true reality. And this position too can be explained by the simile of the hourglass. To be sure, like all similes, it is faulty; but it is precisely through its faults that the essence of time can be demonstrated. Let's see:

An hourglass can be turned over when the upper part has emptied. This, however, cannot be done with time—time is irreversible. Another difference: by shaking the hourglass we can mix up the grains of sand, changing their positions in relation to each other. This we can do with time only in part: we can "shake up" and change the future—and with the future, in the future, we can change even ourselves—but the past is fixed. In terms of the hourglass, it is as if the sand becomes rigid once it has passed through the narrow opening of the present, as if it had been treated by a fixative, a preservative, a conservative. In fact, everything is being conserved in the past, and therein it is conserved forever.

As to the undeniable transitoriness of life, logotherapy contends that this really applies only to the possibilities to fulfill a meaning, the opportunities to create, to experience, and to suffer meaningfully. Once such possibilities have been actualized, they are no longer transitory—they have passed, they *are* past, and that is to say they still exist in a way, namely, as a part of the past. Nothing can change them, nothing can undo them. Once a possibility has been made into a reality, this has been done "once and for all," for all eternity.

Now we may note the sense in which logotherapy counterposes an "optimism of the past" to the "pessimism of the present" propounded by existentialism. I once couched the difference between the two in the following simile: "The pessimist resembles a man who observes with fear and sadness that his wall calendar, from which he daily tears a sheet, grows thinner with each passing day. On the other hand, the person who attacks the problems of life actively is like a man who removes each successive leaf from his calendar and files it neatly and carefully away with its predecessors, after first having jotted down a few diary notes on the back. He can reflect with pride and joy on all the richness set down in these notes, on all the life he has already lived to the full. What will it matter to him if he notices that he is growing old? Has he any reason to envy the young people he sees, or wax nostalgic over his own lost youth? What reasons has he to envy a young person? For the possibilities open to a young person, the future that is in store for him? "No, thank you," he will think. "Instead of possibilities, I have realities in my past, not only the reality of work done and of love loved, but of sufferings bravely suffered. These sufferings are the things of which I am most proud, though these are things which cannot inspire envy."

Young people, for their part, should not let themselves be contaminated by the universal contempt with which a youth-oriented society approaches old people. Otherwise, if the young are lucky enough ever to grow old themselves, they are bound to see their contempt for the old turn into self-contempt.

Logotherapy holds that "having been" is still a mode of being, perhaps even the safest mode. In the phrase "being past," logotherapy places the emphasis on "being." When Martin Heidegger first came to Vienna he visited me at my home and discussed these matters with me. To express his agreement with my view of the past as presented above, he autographed his picture as follows:

> *Das Vergangene geht;*
> *Das Gewesene kommt.*

Or, in my own English translation:

> What has passed, has gone;
> What is past, will come.

Let us now consider the practical applicability of logotherapy's ontology, in particular its ontology of time. Imagine a woman who has lost her husband after only one year of marriage; she is desperate and sees no meaning in her future life. It would mean much to such a person if she now could realize that her one year of marital bliss can never be taken from her. She has rescued it, as it were, into her past. From there, nothing and nobody can ever remove this treasure. Even if she should remain childless her life can never become meaningless once her peak experiences of love have been stored in the storehouse of the past.*

---

* The assumption that procreation is the only meaning of life contradicts and defeats itself; if life is meaningless of itself, it can never be made meaningful merely by its perpetuation.

But, one may ask, is this memory not also transitory? Who, for instance, will keep it alive after the widow dies? To this I would answer that it is irrelevant whether anyone remembers or not; just as it is irrelevant whether we look at or think about something that still exists and is with us. It exists and it continues to exist regardless of whether we look at it or think about it. It continues to exist even irrespective of our own existence.

It is true that we can't take anything with us when we die; but that wholeness of our life, which we complete in the very moment of our death, lies *outside* the grave and outside the grave it *remains*—and it does so, not *although*, but *because* it has slipped into the past. Even what we have forgotten, what has escaped from our consciousness, is not erased from the world; it has become part of the past, and it remains part of the world.

To identify what is part of the past with what anyone still remembers would be a subjectivistic misinterpretation of our ontology of time. This ontology, far from being an ivory-tower affair on a high level of abstraction, can be brought home even to the man in the street if we take a Socratic approach. This happened when I interviewed a patient of mine in class. She had expressed her concern with the transitoriness of life. "Sooner or later it will be over," she said, "and nothing will be left." I could not persuade her that life's transitoriness in no way detracts from its meaningfulness, so I pushed forward by asking her, "Have you ever met a man for whose achievement you have a great respect?" "Certainly," she answered; "our family doctor was a unique person. How he cared for his patients, how he lived for them . . ." "He died?" I inquired. "Yes," she answered. "But his life was exceedingly meaningful, wasn't it?" I asked. "If anyone's life is meaningful, his life was," she said. "But didn't this meaningfulness end at the moment his life was finished?" I asked her. "In no way," she answered; "nothing can alter the fact that his life was meaningful." But I continued challenging her: "And what if not a single patient appreciates what he owes to your family doctor?" "The meaning remains," she murmured. "Or if not a single patient remembers it?" "It remains." "Or when one day the last of his patients has died—?" "It remains . . ."

For another illustration, let me cite a tape-recorded interview I had with another patient of mine.* She was suffering from a terminal cancer, and she knew that she was. When I demonstrated the case in class, the following dialogue developed:

Frankl: What do you think of when you look back on your life? Has life been worth living?
Patient: Well, Doctor, I must say that I had a good life. Life was nice, indeed. And I must thank the Lord for what it held for me: I went to theaters, I attended concerts, and so forth. You see, Doctor, I went there with the family in whose house I served for many decades as a maid, in Prague, at first, and afterward in Vienna. And for the grace of all of these wonderful experiences, I am grateful to the Lord.

------

* See *Modern Psychotherapeutic Practice: Innovations in Technique,* edited by Arthur Burton, Palo Alto, California: Science and Behavior Books, 1965.

I nevertheless felt that she also was doubtful about the ultimate meaning of her life and I wanted to steer her through her doubts, so I had her question the meaning of her life on the conscious level rather than repressing her doubts.

F: You are speaking of some wonderful experiences; but all this will have an end now, won't it?

P: *(thoughtfully):* Yes, everything ends . . .

F: Well, do you think now that all the wonderful things of your life might be annihilated?

P: *(still more thoughtfully):* All those wonderful things . . .

F: But tell me—do you think that anyone can undo the happiness that you have experienced? Can anyone blot it out?

P: No, Doctor, nobody can blot it out!

F: Or can anyone blot out the goodness you have met in your life?

P: *(becoming increasingly emotionally involved):* Nobody can blot it out!

F: What you have achieved and accomplished—

P: Nobody can blot it out!

F: Or what you have bravely and honestly suffered: can anyone remove it from the world—remove it from the past where you have stored it, as it were?

P: *(now moved to tears):* No one can remove it! *[Pause.]* It is true, I have had a great deal to suffer; but I also tried to be courageous and steadfast in enduring what I must. You see, Doctor, I regard my suffering as a punishment. I believe in God.

F: *(trying to put himself in the place of the patient):* But cannot suffering sometimes also be a challenge? Is it not conceivable that God wanted to see how Anastasia Kotek would bear it? And perhaps he had to admit, "Yes, she did so very bravely." And now tell me: can anyone remove such an achievement and accomplishment from the world, Frau Kotek?

P: Certainly no one can do it!

F: This remains, doesn't it?

P: It does!

F: What matters in life is to achieve something. And this is precisely what you have done. You have made the best of your suffering. You have become an example for our patients because of the way you take your suffering upon yourself. I congratulate you for this achievement, and I also congratulate the other patients who have the opportunity to witness such an example. *[To the audience.] Ecce homo! [The audience bursts into spontaneous applause.]* This applause is for you, Frau Kotek. *[She is weeping now.]* It concerns your life, which has been a great achievement. You may be proud of it, Frau Kotek. And how few people may be proud of their lives. . . . I should say, your life is a monument. And no one can remove it from the world.

P: *(regaining her self-control):* What you have said, Professor Frankl, is a consolation. It comforts me. Indeed, I never had an opportunity to hear anything like this. . . . *[Slowly and quietly she leaves the lecture hall.]*

A week later she died. During the last week of her life, however, she was no longer depressed but, on the contrary, full of faith and pride. Prior to this, she had felt agonized, ridden by the anxiety that she was useless. Our interview had made her aware that her life was meaningful and that even her suffering was not in vain. Her last words were: "My life is a monument.

So Professor Frankl said, to the whole audience, to all the students in the lecture hall. My life was not in vain. . . ." (See note on p. 128.)

It is true, everything is transitory—everything and everybody, be it, say, a child we have produced, or the great love from which the child has sprung, or a great thought—they are transitory altogether. Man's life lasts threescore years and ten, possibly fourscore years, and if it is a good life it will have been worth the trouble. A thought may last perhaps seven seconds, and if it is a good thought it will contain truth. But even the great thought still is as transitory as the child and the great love. They are transitory altogether. Everything is transitory.

Yet, on the other hand, everything is eternal. More than that: it becomes eternal of itself. We don't have to do anything about it. Once we have brought something about, eternity will take care of it. But we have to take the responsibility for *what* we have chosen to do, *what* we have selected to become part of the past, *what* we have elected to enter eternity!

Everything is written into the eternal record—our whole life, all our creations and actions, encounters and experiences, all our loving and suffering. All this is contained, and remains, in the eternal record. The world is not, as the great existential philosopher Karl Jaspers intimated, a manuscript written in a code we have to decipher: no, the world is rather a record that we must dictate.

This record is of a dramatic nature, for day by day life is asking us questions, we are interrogated by life, and we have to answer. *Life, I would say, is a life-long question-and-answer period.* As to the answers, I do not weary of saying that we can only answer to life by answering *for* our lives. *Responding* to life means *being responsible* for our lives.

The eternal record cannot be lost—that is a comfort and a hope. But neither can it be corrected—and that is a warning and a reminder. It reminds us that, as nothing can be removed from the past, all the more it is up to us to rescue our chosen possibilities into the past. It now turns out that logotherapy presents not only an "optimism of the past" (in contrast to existentialism's "pessimism of the present") but also an "activism of the future" (in contrast to quietism's "fatalism of eternity"). For if everything is stored in the past forever, it is important to decide in the present what we wish to eternalize by making it part of the past. This is the secret of creativity: that we are moving something from the nothingness of the future into the "being past." Human responsibleness thus rests on the "activism of the future," on one's choosing possibilities from the future, and on the "optimism of the past," that is, turning these possibilities into realities by rescuing them into the haven of the past.

This, then, is the reason everything is so transitory: everything is fleeting because everything is fleeing from the emptiness of the future into the safety of the past! It is as if everything were dominated by what the ancient physicists called the *horror vacui*, the fear of emptiness: that is why everything is rushing from the future into the past, from the vacuum of the future into past existence. That is why there is congestion at the "narrow passage and opening of the present," because there everything is dammed and crowding and waiting to be delivered—as an event passing into the past, or as one of our creations and actions, being admitted by us into eternity.

The present is the borderline between the unreality of the future and the eternal reality of the past. By the same token, it is the "borderline" of eternity; in other words, eternity is finite: it only extends to the present, to the present moment at which we choose what we want to admit into eternity. The borderline of eternity is the place where at every moment of our lives the decision is made as to what should be eternalized and what should not.

We now understand what a mistake it really is to understand the phrase "to gain time" as meant putting things off into the future. Rather, we save time by safely delivering and depositing it in the past.

And what happens, to resume the analogy of the hourglass, when all the sand has run through the neck, and the upper part is empty, when the time has run out on us, and our life has been both finished and finalized? In a word, what happens in death?

In death everything that has passed congeals in the past. Nothing can be changed any more. The person has nothing at his disposal: no mind, no body; he has lost his psychophysical ego. What is left, and what remains, is the self, the spiritual self.

Many people believe that a dying person sees his whole life flash by within a fraction of a second, like a "fast motion" movie.* To pursue this comparison, we may say that in death man becomes the movie himself.

---

* A pertinent story I owe to the late Rudolf Reif, a former mate of mine in rock climbing, and I have also published a paper on the story, together with the late Otto Pötzl, the eminent brain patholo-

He now "is" his life, he has become the history of his life—as good or as bad as it might have been. He has become his own heaven or his own hell.

This leads to the paradox that man's own past is his true future. The living man has both a future and a past; the dying man has no future in the usual sense, but only a past; the dead, however, "is" his past. He has no life, he "is" his life. That it is "only" his *past* life does not matter; after all, the past is the safest mode of being. The past is precisely that which cannot be taken away.

This past is "past perfect" in the literal sense of the term. Life then is perfected, completed. While in the course of life only single *faits accomplis* pass through the neck of the hourglass, now, after death, life in its totality has passed through—has become a *par-fait accompli!*

This leads to a second paradox—a twofold one, at that. If it is true that man, as we said, makes something a reality by putting it into the past (thereby, ironically, *rescuing* it from its transitoriness!)—if this is so, it is man also who makes himself a reality, who "creates" himself. Secondly, he does not become a reality at his birth but rather at his death; he is "creating" himself at the moment of his death. His self is not something that "is" but something that is becoming, and therefore becomes itself fully only when life has been completed by death.

To be sure, in everyday life man is inclined to

---

gist (*"Über die seelischen Zustände während des Absturzes,"* *Monatsschrift für Psychiatrie und Neurologie,* 123, 1952, pp. 362–80).

misunderstand the meaning of death. When the alarm clock goes off in the morning and frightens us from our dreams, we experience this awakening as if something terrible were breaking into the world of our dreams. And, still caught in our dreams, we often do not (at least not immediately) realize that the alarm wakes us up to our real existence, our existence in the real world. But do we mortals not act similarly when we approach death? Do we not equally forget that death awakens us to the true reality of our selves?

Even if a lovingly caressing hand is waking us up—its motion may be ever so gentle, but we do not realize its gentleness. Again, we only experience an intrusion upon the world of our dreams, an attempt to finish them off. Likewise more often than not death appears to be something dreadful, and we hardly suspect how well it is meant. . . .

NOTE: Terry E. Zuehlke and John T. Watkins have "investigated the effectiveness of logotherapy with terminally ill patients. The patients experienced a significant increase in their sense of purpose and meaning in their lives as measured by the Purpose in Life Test." (T. E. Zuehlke & J. T. Watkins, "The Use of Psychotherapy with Dying Patients: An Exploratory Study." *Journal of Clinical Psychology,* 1975, 31, pp. 729–732. And T. E. Zuehlke & J. T. Watkins, "Psychotherapy with Terminally Ill Patients." *Psychotherapy: Theory, Research and Practice,* 1977, 14, pp. 403–410.)

Paradoxical Intention
and Dereflection

PARADOXICAL INTENTION AND DEREFLECTION ARE
two techniques developed within the framework of
logotherapy (Frankl, 1938, 1955, 1958; Polak, 1949;
Weisskopf-Joelson, 1955). Logotherapy is usually
either subsumed under the category of humanistic
psychology (Buhler and Allen, 1972), or identified with
phenomenological (Spiegelberg, 1972) or existential
psychiatry (Allport, 1959; Lyons, 1961; Pervin, 1960).
It is the contention of several authors, however, that
logotherapy is the only one of these systems that has
succeeded in developing psychotherapeutic techniques in the proper sense of the word (Leslie, 1965;
Kaczanowski, 1965, 1967; Tweedie, 1961; Ungersma,
1961). The techniques they refer to are those I have
termed "paradoxical intention" (Frankl, 1947, 1955)
and "dereflection" (Frankl, 1947, 1955).

PARADOXICAL INTENTION

I have used paradoxical intention since 1929, although I did not publish a formal description of it until

1939. Later on, it was elaborated into a methodology (Frankl, 1953) and incorporated into the system of logotherapy (Frankl, 1956). Since then the growing literature on paradoxical intention has shown the technique to be an effective therapy in cases of obsessive-compulsive and phobic conditions (Gerz, 1962; Kaczanowski, 1965; Kocourek, Niebauer and Polak, 1959; Lehembre, 1964; Medlicott, 1969; Muller-Hegemann, 1963; Victor and Krug, 1967; Weisskopf-Joelson, 1968), in which it often proves to be a short-term treatment (Dilling *et al.*, 1971; Gerz, 1966; Henkel *et al.*, 1972; Jacobs, 1972; Marks, 1969, 1972; Solyom *et al.*, 1972).

To understand how paradoxical intention works, take as a starting point the mechanism called anticipatory anxiety: a given symptom evokes on the part of the patient the fearful expectation that it might recur. Fear, however, always tends to bring about precisely that which is feared, and by the same token, anticipatory anxiety is liable and likely to trigger off what the patient so fearfully expects to happen. Thus a self-sustaining vicious circle is established: a symptom evokes a phobia; the phobia provokes the symptom;

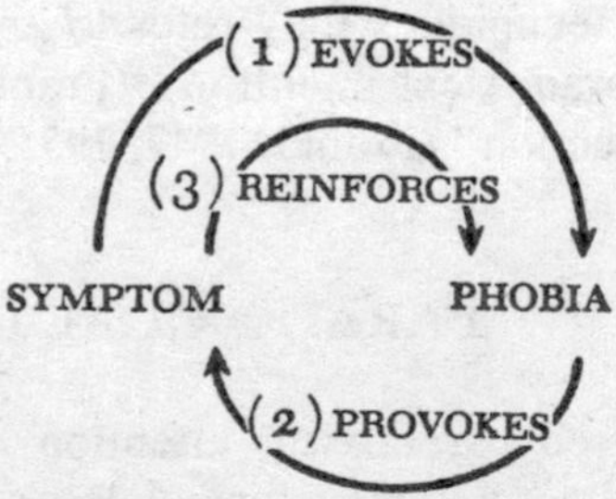

FIGURE 1

and the recurrence of the symptom reinforces the phobia.

One object of fear is fear itself: our patients often refer to "anxiety about anxiety." Upon closer scrutiny, this "fear of fear" frequently turns out to be caused by the patient's apprehensions about the potential effects of his anxiety attacks: he is afraid that they may eventuate in his collapsing or fainting, or in a heart attack, or in a stroke. But, alas, the fear of fear increases fear.

The most typical reaction to "fear of fear" is "flight from fear" (Frankl, 1953): the patient begins to avoid those situations that used to arouse his anxiety. In other words, he runs away from his fear. This is the starting point of any anxiety neurosis: "Phobias are partially due to the endeavour to avoid the situation in which anxiety arises" (Frankl, 1960). Learning theorists and behavior therapists have since confirmed this finding. It is the contention of Marks (1970), for example, that "the phobia is maintained by the anxiety-reducing mechanism of avoidance." Contrariwise, "the development of a phobia can be obviated by confronting one with the situation he begins to fear" (Frankl, 1969).

"Flight from fear" as a reaction to "fear of fear" constitutes the *phobic pattern,* the first of three pathogenic patterns that are distinguished in logotherapy (Frankl, 1953). The second is the *obsessive-compulsive* pattern: whereas in phobic cases the patient displays "fear of fear," the obsessive-compulsive neurotic exhibits "fear of himself," being either caught by the idea that he might commit suicide—or even homicide—or afraid that the strange thoughts that haunt him might be signs of imminent, if not present, psychosis. How should he know that the obsessive-compulsive character structure rather is immunizing him against real psychosis (Frankl, 1955)?

While "flight from fear" is a characteristic of the phobic pattern, the obsessive-compulsive patient is characterized by his "fight against obsessions and compulsions." But alas, the more he fights them the stronger they become: pressure induces counterpressure, and counterpressure, in turn, increases pressure.* Again, we are confronted with a vicious circle.

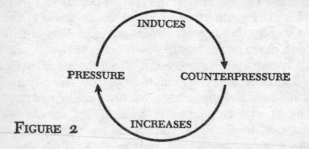

FIGURE 2

How then is it possible to break up such feedback mechanism? And to begin with, how can we take the wind out of the individual fears of our patients? Well, this is precisely the business to accomplish by paradoxical intention, which may be defined as a process by which *the patient is encouraged to do, or to wish to happen, the very thing he fears* (the former applying to the phobic patient, the latter to the obsessive-compulsive). In this way, we have the phobic patient stop

---

* This is most conspicuous in cases of blasphemous obsessions. For a technique to treat them specifically, see Frankl, 1955.

fleeing from his fears, and the obsessive-compulsive patient stop fighting his obsessions and compulsions. In any way, the pathogenic fear now is replaced by a paradoxical wish. The vicious circle of anticipatory anxiety is now unhinged.

For illustrative case material, the reader is referred to the pertinent literature (Frankl, 1955, 1962, 1967, 1969; Gerz, 1962, 1966; Jacobs, 1972; Kaczanowski, 1965; Medlicott, 1969; Solyom *et al.*, 1972; Victor and Krug, 1967; Weisskopf-Joelson, 1968). Here only unpublished material is quoted, the first an unsolicited letter I once received from a reader.

> I had to take an examination yesterday and discovered ½ hour beforehand that I was literally frozen with fear. I looked at my notes and my mind blanked out. The things I had studied so long looked completely unfamiliar to me and I panicked: "I don't remember *anything!* I will fail this test!" Needless to say, my fear increased as the minutes went by, my notes looked more and more unfamiliar, I was sweating, and my fear was building each time I rechecked those notes! *Five minutes* before the examination I knew that if I felt this way during the exam I would surely fail; and then your paradoxical intention came to my mind. I said to myself, "Since I am going to fail anyway, I may as well *do my best at failing!* I'll show this professor a test *so* bad, that it will confuse him for days! I will write down total garbage, answers that have nothing to do with the questions at all! I'll show him how a student really fails a test! This will be the most ridiculous test he grades in his entire career!" With this in mind, I was actually giggling when the exam came. Believe it or not, each question made perfect sense to me—I was relaxed, at ease, and as strange as it may sound, actually in a terrific mood! I passed the test and received an

A. P. S. Paradoxical intention also cures the hiccups.
If one *tries* to keep hiccuping, one can't!

The following excerpt, from another letter, may serve as another illustration:

> I am forty years old, and I have been suffering from a neurosis for at least ten years. I sought psychiatric help but did not find the relief that I had looked for (I had about eighteen months of therapy). After one of your lectures in 1968 I heard one of the men asking you how to treat his fear of flying. I listened all the more carefully since this was also my phobia. With what I assume to have been your "paradoxical intention" technique, you told him to let the plane explode and crash and see himself crushed to bits in it! Scarely a month later I was to fly about 2500 miles, and as usual I was scared. My hands were sweaty and my heart was palpitating, and your prescription to the other man came to mind. So I imagined that the plane exploded; I was tumbling through the clouds, headed for the ground. Before I could finish the fantasy, I realized that I was suddenly thinking very calmly about some of the business I had transacted. I tried several more times until I managed to splatter myself in a bloody heap on the ground. When the plane landed I was calm and even enjoying an eagle's view of the land. Being a Freudian in training and therapy, I have found myself wondering about the deeper levels of one's pathology that paradoxical intention does not touch. Yet I am now wondering if there are not therapeutic resources that are even deeper than the pathological ones, resources that are basically human and that can be released by paradoxical intention.

Another case, compulsive rather than phobic in nature, was reported by Darrell Burnett, a counselor:

A man came to the community mental health center complaining of a compulsion he had to check the front door at night before he went to bed. He had reached the point where he was checking and rechecking the door ten times within a two-minute span. He said he had tried in vain to talk himself out of it, but to no avail. I asked him to see how many times he could check the door within the two-minute span, to try to set a new record! At first he thought it was silly, but after three days the compulsion had disappeared.

For another case report, I am indebted to Larry Ramirez:

The technique that has helped me most often and worked most effectively in my counseling sessions is paradoxical intention. For example, Linda T., an attractive nineteen-year-old college student, had indicated on her appointment card that she was having some problems at home with her parents. As we sat down, it was quite evident to me that she was very tense. She stuttered. My natural reaction would have been to say, "Relax, it's all right," or "Just take it easy," but from past experience I knew that asking her to relax would only serve to increase her tension. Instead, I responded with just the opposite, "Linda, I want you to be as tense as you possibly can. Act as nervously as you can." "O.K." she said, "being nervous is easy for me." She started by clenching her fists together and shaking her hands as though they were trembling. "That's good," I said, "but try to be more nervous." The humor of the situation became obvious to her and she said, "I really was nervous, but I can't be any longer. It's odd, but the more I try to be tense, the less I'm able to be." In recalling this case, it is evident to me that it was the humor that came from using paradoxical intention that helped Linda realize that she was a human being first and foremost and a client second, and that I too was first a person and her counselor second. Humor best illustrated our humanness.

The role of humor in the practice of paradoxical intention becomes even more obvious in the following quotation, from a paper by Mohammed Sadiq:

Mrs. N., a forty-eight-year-old lady diagnosed as hysteric, had body shaking and trembling. She would have trembling fits to the extent that she was not able to hold a cup of coffee without spilling it over and over. She could not write or hold a book firmly enough to read. One morning she came out of her room and was sitting in front of me on the other side of the table when she started trembling and shaking. There were no other patients around, so I decided to use paradoxical intention in a really humorous way.

Therapist: How would you like to compete with me in shaking, Mrs. N.?
Patient (shocked): What?
T.: Let us see who can shake and tremble faster and for how long?
P.: Are you suffering from these shakes too?
T.: No, I am not suffering from them, but I can tremble if I want to. [I began to shake.]
P.: Gee. You are doing it faster. [Trying to speed up and smiling.]
T.: Faster. Come on, Mrs. N., faster.
P.: I can't. [She was becoming tired.] Quit it. I can't do it any more. [She got up, went in the day room, and brought herself a cup of coffee. She drank the whole cup without spilling it once.]
T.: That was fun, wasn't it?

Afterwards, whenever I would see her shaking I would say, "Come on, Mrs. N., let's have a race," and she would say, "O.K. It sure works."

Indeed, it is essential in practicing paradoxical intention to do what Ramirez and Sadiq did, namely, to mobilize and utilize the exclusively human capacity for humor. Lazarus (1971) points out that "an integral element in Frankl's paradoxical intention procedure is the deliberate evocation of humor. A patient who fears that he may perspire is enjoined to show his audience what perspiration is really like, to perspire in gushes of drenching torrents of sweat which will moisturize everything within touching distance." Raskin and Klein (1976) ask the question: "What more powerful manner to minimize a complaint than, with a twinkle, to endorse it?" However, we should not forget that the sense of humor is exclusively human—after all, no animal but man is capable of laughing. Specifically, humor is to be regarded as a manifestation of that peculiarly human ability which in logotherapy is called self-detachment (Frankl, 1966). No longer is it tenable to deplore, as Lorenz did (1967), "that we do not as yet take humor seriously enough." We logotherapists have been doing so, I dare say, since 1929. It is most noteworthy in this context that recently even the behavior therapists have come to recognize the importance of humor. To quote Hand *et al.* (1974), who "treated patients with chronic agoraphobia effectively by group exposure *in vivo,*" it was observed that "an impressive coping device used by the groups was humor (*vide* the paradoxical intention of Frankl, 1960). This was used spontaneously and often helped to overcome difficult situations. When the whole group was frightened, somebody would break the ice with a joke, which would be greeted with the laughter of relief."

As logotherapy teaches, the capacity of self-detachment—along with another, the capacity of self-transcendence (Frankl, 1959)—is an intrinsically and definitely human phenomenon, and as such eludes any reductionist attempt to trace it back to subhuman phenomena. By virtue of self-detachment man is capable of joking about himself, laughing at himself, and ridiculing his own fears. By virtue of his capacity of self-transcendence, he is capable of forgetting himself, giving himself, and reaching out for a meaning to his existence. To be sure, he then is also liable to be frustrated in his search for meaning, but this too is understandable only on the human level. Psychiatric approaches that stick either to "the machine model" or to "the rat model," as Gordon Allport (1960) called them, give away therapeutic assets. After all, no computer is capable of laughing at itself, nor is a rat capable of asking itself whether its existence has a meaning.

This criticism does not deny the importance of learning theoretical concepts and behavior-therapeutic approaches. As compared with behavior therapy, logotherapy simply adds another dimension—the distinctively human dimension—and thus is in a position to muster resources that are available only in the human dimension. Seen in this light, the Norwegian psychologist Bjarne Kvilhaug (1963) was justified in contending that logotherapy might accomplish what he called the "humanization" of behavior therapy.

Behavioristically oriented research in turn has empirically corroborated and validated much of logotherapeutic practice and theory. As Agras (1972) sees it, "paradoxical intention effectively exposes the patient to his feared situation by asking him deliberately to try to bring on the feared consequences of his behavior instead of avoiding situations. Thus, the agoraphobic with a fear that she will faint if she walks alone is told to try and faint. She finds she cannot and is enabled to confront her phobic situation." Even prior to this observation, Lazarus (1971) had pointed out that "when people encourage their anticipatory anxieties to erupt, they nearly always find the opposite reaction coming to the fore—their worst fears subside and when the method is used several times, their dreads eventually disappear." Dilling, Rosefeldt, Kockott and Heyse (1971) contend that "the good, and sometimes very fast, results obtained by paradoxical intention can be explained along the lines of learning theory."*

---

* In view of all the similarities between logotherapy and behavior therapy one should not overlook or dismiss the differences. I am indebted to Elizabeth Bedoya to whom I owe a story that illustrates the difference between the logotherapeutic technique of paradoxical intention on one hand and on the other hand the token economy which is representative of behavior modification: "Mr. and Mrs. . . . were very upset with their nine year old son, who still wet the bed every night. They asked my father for advice, and told him of how they spanked him, talked to him, embarrassed him, ignored him, etc. But nothing they said or did made him stop wetting the bed, he only became worse. My father told him that for every night he wet the bed, he would receive a nickel. Rudy promised to take me to the movies and buy me a candy-bar, he knew that he would have plenty of money left over. But, on the next visit, Rudy could only report earning two nickels. He told my father that he tried very hard to wet

Lapinsohn (1971) tried to interpret the results obtained by paradoxical intention even on neurophysiological grounds, an explanation which is as legitimate as that attempted by Muller-Hegemann (1963), whose orientation is basically reflexological. This is in accordance with an interpretation of neurosis that I offered in 1947:

> All psychoanalytically oriented psychotherapies are mainly concerned with uncovering the primary conditions of the "conditioned reflex" as which neurosis may well be understood, namely, the situation—outer and inner—in which a given neurotic symptom emerged the first time. It is this author's contention, however, that the fullfledged neurosis is caused not only by the primary conditions but also by secondary conditioning. This reinforcement, in turn, is caused by the feedback mechanism called anticipatory anxiety. Therefore, if we wish to recondition a conditioned reflex, we must unhinge the vicious cycle formed by anticipatory anxiety, and this is the very job done by our paradoxical intention technique.

Behavior therapists have not only come up with explanations of how paradoxical intention works, but also have set out to prove experimentally that it really does work. Solyom *et al.* (1972) successfully treated chronically ill patients who had suffered from obsessive neurosis from four to twenty-five years. One had had a four-and-a-half-year psychoanalysis; four had had electroshock treatment. The authors chose two

the bed each night, because he wanted to earn a lot of money. He was very sad, and could not understand what happened, he never failed before!"

symptoms that were approximately equal both in importance to the patient and in frequency of occurrence, and applied paradoxical intention to one. The other, the "control thought," was left untreated. Although the treatment period was short (six weeks), there was an improvement rate of 50% in the target thoughts. "Some subjects later reported that after the experimental period they had successfully applied paradoxical intention to other obsessive thoughts." At the same time, "there was no symptom substitution." The authors conclude that "paradoxical intention alone, or in combination with other treatments, may be a relatively fast method for some obsessive patients."

As a matter of fact, the literature on paradoxical intention includes cases in which this logotherapeutic technique was combined with behavior modification, and some behavior therapists have demonstrated that the therapeutic effects obtained by behavior therapy can be enhanced by the addition of logotherapeutic techniques such as paradoxical intention. It is in line with this sound eclecticism that Jacobs (1972) cites the case of Mrs. K., who for fifteen years had suffered from severe claustrophobia:

> The phobia extended to flying in aircraft, traveling in elevators, being in trains, buses, cinemas, restaurants, theaters, department stores and other closed, confined spaces. . . . The problem was particularly debilitating since Mrs. K., who lived in Britain, was an actress and was often required to fly abroad in order to act on stage and television. . . . The patient presented herself for treatment eight days before being due to leave South Africa, where she was holidaying, to return to Britain. . . . She feared she would choke or die. . . . She was then taught thought

stopping and told to use this to block out any "catastrophic thoughts." Frankl's technique of paradoxical intention was then brought in to further attack her cognitions and behavioral responses to the phobias. She was told that whenever she began to feel anxious in any of the phobic situations, instead of trying to fight and suppress the symptoms and thoughts which troubled her, she was to say to herself, "I know there is nothing physically wrong with me, I'm only tense and hyperventilating, in fact I want to prove this to myself by letting these symptoms become as bad as possible." She was told to try to suffocate or die "right on the spot" and to try to exaggerate her physical symptoms. She was then taught a brief modified form of Jacobson's progressive relaxation. She was told to practice it and to apply it in the phobic situations to remain calm, but it was stressed that she should not try too hard to relax or fight the tension. While under relaxation, desensitization was begun. . . . Before the patient left the consulting room, she was instructed to seek out all the previous phobic situations, such as elevators, crowded stores, cinemas, restaurants, initially with her husband, then alone; place herself in them and to do the following: to relax as taught, hold her breath if she hyperventilated, to tell herself to let it come, "I don't care, I can handle it, let it do its damnedest, I want to prove that nothing happens." . . . She was seen two days later and reported that she had carried out her instructions, that she had been in a cinema and restaurant, had traveled innumerable times in elevators alone, and had been in several buses and crowded stores. . . . The patient was seen four days later, just prior to her departure by plane for Britain. She had maintained her improvement and was feeling no anticipatory anxiety whatsoever regarding the flight she was about to undertake. She reported, and her husband confirmed, that she had been in elevators, buses, crowded stores, in a restaurant and cinema, etc. without any anxiety or fear. . . . The patient wrote to me, the letter being received two weeks after she had left South Africa. She reported that she had had no difficulty at all during the flight home and she had been completely free of her phobias. She had also been traveling on London subway trains—which she had not done for many years. I saw Mrs. K. and her husband 15 months after the termination of her treatment. Both confirm that she has remained completely free of her previous symptoms.

Jacobs also describes the treatment of another patient, who was compulsive rather than phobic. Mr. T. had suffered a debilitating obsessive-compulsive neurosis for twelve years. A variety of treatments, including psychoanalytically oriented therapy and E.C.T., had failed to help.

[He had] over the previous 7 years developed an obsession and fear about choking, so that he found it difficult to eat or drink as he became extremely anxious and in trying to force himself to swallow had produced a state of globus hystericus. He found it difficult to cross a road as he thought he might choke when halfway across it. . . . He was then instructed to deliberately set about doing the very things he had so feared and which his obsessions were meant to obviate, until they no longer bothered him. . . . The patient was also instructed to practice relaxation whenever eating, drinking or crossing roads. Using the technique of paradoxical intention, he was given a glass of water to drink and told to try as hard as possible to make himself choke—which he was quite unable to do. He was instructed to try to choke at least 3 times a day. . . . The next few sessions were devoted to further anxiety reduction techniques and the use of paradoxical intention. . . . By the 12th session the patient was able to report the complete disappearance of his former obsessions.

Another pertinent report reads as follows:

Vicki, a junior in high school, came into my counseling office. She cried and said she was flunking speech although she was a straight A student in all her other courses. I asked her why or whether she had an idea why she was flunking. She said that each time she stood up to make a speech she became more and more afraid to the point that she couldn't give any speeches, or stand up in class. She had many signs of anticipatory anxiety. I then suggested role-playing, she the speaker and I the audience. I used behavior modification techniques, with positive reinforcement, each time we role-played on 3 days. She set the goal that after her first successful speech in class she would receive an off-campus pass, something she wanted very much. The next day she could not make her speech in class and came into my office sobbing. Since behavior modification approaches had failed, I tried paradoxical intention. I firmly told Vicki that the next day she would show the whole class how fearful she was; she should cry, sob, shake and perspire as much as possible, and I demonstrated. During her speech she attempted to demonstrate how fearful she was but could not. Instead she gave a speech that her teacher graded A.

Also Barbara W. Martin, a high school counselor, has "first used the behavior modification techniques, and later found logotherapeutic techniques much more successful and helpful in working with high school students." Milton E. Burglass of the Orleans Parish Prison Department of Rehabilitation even instituted an experimental program of 72 hours of therapeutic counseling. Four groups of 16 subjects each were established. One group was selected as a control group to receive no therapy at all; one group was assigned to a psychiatrist trained in Freudian analysis; one group was assigned to a psychologist trained in behavior or learning therapy; and one group was assigned to a therapist trained in logotherapy. "Post-therapeutic interviews revealed a general dissatisfaction with the Freudian therapy, a rather apathetic attitude toward the behavior therapy, and a quite positive feeling about logotherapy and the benefits derived therefrom."

What is true of the behavioristically oriented approaches holds true for the psychodynamically oriented ones. Some psychoanalysts not only use paradoxical intention, but also try to explain its success in Freudian terms (Gerz, 1966; Havens, 1968; Weisskopf-Joelson, 1955). More recently, Harrington, in an unpublished paper, expressed the conviction that "paradoxical intention is an attempt to consciously initiate the automatic defense erecting counterphobic attitude described by Fenichel. In a psychoanalytic model, paradoxical intention may be viewed as relieving symptoms by utilizing defenses which require less expenditure of psychic energy than the phobic or obsessive-compulsive symptom itself. Each time paradoxical intention is successfully applied, the id impulses are gratified, the superego becomes an ally to the ego, and the ego itself gains strength and becomes less restricted. This results in decreased anxiety and diminished symptom formation."

Paradoxical intention is used not only by psychoanalysts and behavior therapists, but also by psychiatrists who combine it with suggestive treatment. An instance of this was reported by Briggs (1970) at a meeting of the Royal Society of Medicine:

> I was asked to see a young man from Liverpool, a stutterer. He wanted to take up teaching, but stuttering and teaching do not go together. His greatest fear and worry was his embarrassment by the stuttering so that he went through mental agonies every time he had to say anything. He used to have a kind of mental rehearsal of everything he was going to say, and then try to say it. Then he would become frightfully embarrassed about it. It seemed logical that if this young man could be enabled to do something which previously he had been afraid to do it might work. I remembered a short time before having read an article by Viktor Frankl, who wrote about a reaction of paradox. I then gave the following suggestions—"You are going out into the world this week-end and you are going to show people what a jolly good stutterer you are. And you are going to fail in this just as you have failed in the previous years to speak properly." He came up the following week and was obviously elated because his speech was so much better. He said, "What do you think happened! I went into a pub with some friends and one of them said to me I thought you used to be a stutterer and I said I did—so what!" It was successful. I don't claim any credit for this case; if it should go to anyone but the patient it should go to Viktor Frankl.

Briggs combined paradoxical intention with suggestion deliberately; but suggestion cannot be completely eliminated from therapy, anyway. Still it would be a mistake to dismiss the therapeutic success of paradoxical intention as a merely suggestive effect. The following report, concerning another case of stuttering, might cast some light on this issue. It was written by a student at Duquesne University:

For seventeen years I stuttered very severely; at times I could not speak at all. I saw many speech therapists, but had no success. One of my instructors assigned your book, *Man's Search for Meaning,* to be read for a course. So, I read the book and I decided to try paradoxical intention by myself. The very first time I tried it, it worked fabulously—no stuttering. I then sought out other situations in which I would normally stutter, and I applied paradoxical intention and it successfully alleviated stuttering in those situations. There were a couple of situations thereafter when I did not use paradoxical intention— and the stuttering quickly returned. This is a definite proof that the alleviation of my stuttering problem was due to the effective use of paradoxical intention.

Its use may even be effective in cases where negative suggestion was involved, that is to say, when the patient did in no way "believe" in the effectiveness of the treatment. Let us take up, as an example, the following report delivered by Abraham George Pynummootil, a social worker:

A young man came to my office with a severe case of eye winking problem. He was winking his eyes in a rapid fashion whenever he had to talk to someone. People began to ask him why he was doing so and he began to worry about it. I advised him to consult a psychoanalyst. After many hours of consultation he came back saying the psychoanalyst could not find the reason for his problem and that he could not help to solve the problem. I told him, the next time when you talk to someone wink your eyes as rapidly as possible and as fast as you can deliberately to show that person just how much more you can really wink your eyes. He said that I must be crazy to suggest this to him for he thought that he will get more into the habit of winking his eyes rather than get out of it. So he stomped out of my room. I did not hear from or see him for a few weeks. Then one day, he came again. This time he was full of joy and told me what happened. As he did not agree with my suggestion, he did not think about it for a few days. During this time his problem became worse and he was almost going out of his mind. One night as he was going to bed, he thought about my suggestion and said to himself, "I have tried everything I know to get out of this problem but failed. Why don't I try the one thing the social worker suggested?" So the next day, it just happened that the first person he met was a close friend. He told him that he was going to wink his eyes as much as he could when he talked to him. But to his surprise, he could not wink his eyes at all when talking to him. From then on he became normal in his eye winking habit. After a few weeks he did not even think about it at all.

Benedikt (1968) administered batteries of tests to patients for whom paradoxical intention had been successful, in order to evaluate their susceptibility to suggestion. It turned out that they were even less susceptible than the average. Moreover, many patients set out to use paradoxical intention with a strong conviction that it cannot work, but eventually they succeed. They do so not because but rather in spite of suggestion. As an example, take the following report, from another of my readers:

Two days after reading *Man's Search for Meaning,* a situation arose which offered the opportunity to put logotherapy to the test. During the first meeting of a seminar class on Martin Buber, I spoke up saying I felt diametrically opposed to the views so far expressed. While expressing my views I began to perspire heavily. When I became aware of my excessive sweating I felt even more anxiety about the others seeing me perspire, and this caused me to sweat even more. Almost instantly I recalled a case study of a physician who consulted you, Dr. Frankl, because of his fear of perspiring, and I thought, "Here I am in a similar situation." Being ever skeptical of methods, and specifically of logotherapy, in this instance I determined the situation was ideal for a trial and put logotherapy to the test. I remembered your advice to the physician and resolved to deliberately show those people how much I could sweat, chanting in my thoughts as I continued to express my feelings on the subject: "More! More! More! Show these people how much you can sweat, really show them!" Within two or three seconds after applying paradoxical intention I laughed inwardly and could feel the sweat beginning to dry on my skin. I was amazed and surprised at the result, for I did not believe logotherapy would work. It did, and so quickly! Again, inwardly, I said to myself, "Damn, that Dr. Frankl really has something here! Regardless of my skeptical feelings, logotherapy actually worked in my case." (See note on p. 184.)

Paradoxical intention can also be successfully used with children (Lehembre, 1964), even in a classroom setting. I owe a pertinent illustration to Pauline Furness, a counselor and elementary school teacher:

Libby (11 years old) constantly stared at certain other children. These children complained to Libby, threatened her and all to no avail. Miss H., Libby's teacher, insisted that Libby must stop staring at the other children. The teacher had tried behavior modification techniques, isolation punishment and one-to-one counseling. The situation became worse. Miss H. was most helpful and we formulated a plan of action. The next day before school she called Libby to the room and said, "Libby, today I want you to stare at Ann and Richard and Lois. First one and then the other for fifteen minutes each all day long. If you forget, I'll remind you. No classwork, only staring. Won't that be fun?" Libby eyed Miss H. quizzically, "B . . . b . . . but, Miss H., that sounds goofy." "Not at all, Libby, I am really serious," Miss H. replied. "It seems so silly," Libby replied, smiling slightly. Now Miss H. broke out in a wide grin, "It does seem ridiculous, doesn't it? Want to give it a try?" Libby blushed. Miss H. then explained that sometimes if we force ourselves to do something we don't want to do it breaks the habit. The class filed in and when all were seated Miss H. gave Libby the secret signal to begin. Libby looked at Miss H. for a moment and then came up to her and pleaded, "I just can't do it!" "O.K.," said Miss H., "we'll try again later." By the end of the day Miss H. and Libby were both delighted at Libby's inability to stare. For eight successive days Miss H. started each morning with this question to Libby privately, "Want to try staring today?" The answer was always "No!" Libby never fell back into her behavior pattern of staring. She was proud of her achievement and later in the term asked Miss H. if she noticed that the staring had stopped. Miss H. said she had and congratulated Libby. In our final consultation about Libby, Miss H. reported to me that Libby had gained stature with classmates and a much improved self-image. I enjoy working with paradoxical intention because it offers a theme of "Let's not take life so seriously. Let's make fun out of our problems. If we can stand aside and peek at them and laugh at them, they will go away, pooh!" I often say this to the children and they capture the spirit of the jest.

And, we may say, she captured the spirit of our technique, which rests on man's capacity for self-detachment.

Such cases are not intended to suggest that paradoxical intention is effective in every case, or that its effect is easy to obtain. Neither paradoxical intention in particular nor logotherapy in general is a panacea—panaceas simply do not exist in the field of psychotherapy. Paradoxical intention may, though, be effective even in severe and chronic cases, in old age as well as in childhood. In this connection ample material has been published by Kocourek, Niebauer and Polak (1959), Gerz (1962, 1966) and Victor and Krug (1967). One of the cases reported by Niebauer was a sixty-five-year-old woman who had suffered from a hand-washing compulsion for sixty years; Gerz treated a woman who had a twenty-four-year history of phobic neurosis; and the case treated by Victor and Krug was one of compulsive gambling that had lasted for twenty years. Even in these cases success could be obtained. To be sure, in such cases success is available only at the expense of total personal involvement on the part of the therapist. This is demonstrated in detail by a report on an obsessive-compulsive lawyer treated by Kocourek, which was published by Friedrich M. Benedikt and constituted part of his dissertation at the University of Munich Medical School:*

> The case concerns a 41-year-old lawyer, who retired early because of his obsessive-compulsive neurosis. His father had a bacteriophobia which may indicate a hereditary facet of his illness.† As a child, the patient used to open doors with his elbows from fear of possible contamination (European doors have handles that have to be pushed down, not twisted

---

* For the translation of the following report from the German into English, I am indebted to Dr. Joseph B. Fabry, Director of the Institute of Logotherapy, at Berkeley.

† I subscribe to the conviction of Hays (1972) that "genetic predisposition is almost a sine qua non," at least as far as severe cases are concerned.

like American doorknobs). He was overly concerned with cleanliness and avoided contact with other children because they might have been disease carriers. During his elementary and high school years he remained isolated. He was shy and his schoolmates teased him because he was so withdrawn. The patient recalls one of the first symptoms of his illness. In 1938, walking home one night, he found a postcard he felt compelled to read six times. "If I hadn't read it, I would have found no peace." Evenings he felt compelled to read books until "everything was in order." He avoided bananas which, coming from primitive countries, he associated with harboring bacteria, especially those of leprosy. In 1939 he began to suffer from a "Good Friday craze," a fear he might have unknowingly eaten meat or violated some other religious rule. In high school, while discussing Kant's *Critique of Pure Reason,* he was exposed to the thought that the objects of this world may not be real. "This sentence was the truly decisive blow for me, all else had been only a prelude," he complained. It became the central theme of his illness. The patient began worrying about doing everything "one hundred percent" correctly.* He constantly kept searching his conscience, according to a strict ritual. "I established a formalism," he stated, "which I still have to observe." He felt compelled to make a wide detour around every cross, for fear of touching something holy. He began to repeat certain phrases, such as "I have done nothing wrong," to escape punishment. During the war his symptoms somewhat receded. His comrades teased him about not going with them to brothels. He had remained sexually naive and did not know that intercourse required an erection. One girl told him that there was something wrong with him because he

---

*For "hundred-percentness" as a constitutive feature of the obsessive-compulsive character structure, see Frankl (1955).

lacked masculine aggression. Some psychoanalytical treatment and hypnosis proved successful inasmuch as he achieved an erection. These treatments, however, did not make his obsessive-compulsive symptoms disappear. In 1949 he married. Initial trouble with potency disappeared after renewed treatment. By that time he had concluded his studies and graduated from the university. He worked for the police force and later in the Ministry of Finance, but lost his job because he was slow and inefficient. Renewed consultation with the doctor brought no improvement. He found a job with the railroad. During this period he did not allow his daughter to come near him because he was afraid he might abuse her sexually. His obsessive-compulsive symptoms increased since 1953. In 1956 he read about a schizophrenic nurse who had gouged out her own eyeballs. He began to fear that he might do the same to himself or to small children. *"The more I fought the thought the worse it became,"* he stated. Numbers took on significance. At night he felt obligated to put three oranges on the table, or he couldn't find any rest. Again he changed jobs. In 1960 he received treatment from a psychologist but treatments were unsuccessful. In 1961 treatment by a homeopath and acupuncture both failed. In 1962 he became a patient in a mental hospital, where he received 45 insulin shocks after he was diagnosed a schizophrenic. The night before dismissal he suffered a breakdown, and he was overwhelmed by the thought that everything was unreal. "From that day on," the patient stated, "this central theme of my illness has been threatening me and I have been in deep trouble." Treatments abroad followed. Within one year he changed jobs 20 times, including such jobs as tourist guide, ticket agent, and printer's helper. In 1963 he received work therapy, which he considered at least partly successful. However, from 1964 on, his obsessive-compulsive symptoms become stronger and he is unable to work. His most frequent thought during this period is "I might have gouged out somebody's eyes. I have to turn around every time I pass someone on the street to make sure I didn't do it." His illness became unbearable for his family. He was admitted to the Poliklinik with a diagnosis of "severe obsessive-compulsive neurosis." The examination revealed no organic disturbances. Drug treatments were given to the patient to calm him. Day 1 of the psychotherapeutic treatment: The patient is restless, tense, keeps looking at the door to see if he has not gouged out anybody's eyes. He makes a wide detour around each child in the corridor who is passing by from the nearby nose-ear-and-throat clinic. He constantly goes through certain "ceremonial" motions to make sure he has not hurt anyone. He keeps looking at his hands, fearful that he might have gouged out eyes so that vitreous humor was drained. Day 2 initiates a long and rather general discussion, which is continued during the entire period of treatment. Dr. Kocourek concentrates his efforts on the patient's guilt feelings, his relationship to his mother, wife, and children, his continuous changing of jobs, his obsession that everything is unreal, and such. When the patient expressed his fear that he would end up in an institution or that he would be driven to attack children and then be locked up as "insane," Dr. Kocourek explained to him the difference between a compulsive action and an obsessive thought. He then pointed out to the patient that exactly because of his illness he was unable to hurt anyone. His illness, being an obsessive-compulsive neurosis, was a guarantee that he would not commit criminal acts: his very fear that he might gouge out other people's eyes was the reason that he would be unable to carry out his obsessive thought. On day 4 the patient seems more quiet and relaxed. Day 5: The patient is not certain, he says, that he understood everything correctly. Again and again he demands assurances that the explanations of Dr. Kocourek are valid "everywhere in the whole world and at all times." Days 6 to 10: The conversations with the patient are continued. He asks many questions, which are answered in detail. He appears to be less anxious than on previous days. Day 11: The essence of paradoxical intention is explained to the patient: he is not to repress his thoughts but rather to let them well up in him; they will not result in the actions he fears. He is to try to meet his thoughts with irony, or to meet them "with humor"—then he will no longer fear his obsessive thoughts, and if he does not fight them, they will fade away. Whatever he fears he should plan to actually do—as an obsessive-compulsive neurotic he could afford to do that. Dr. Kocourek himself would take the responsibility for whatever the patient would do. Day 15: The active exercises begin. Accompanied by Dr. Kocourek, Herr H. walks through the hospital, practicing paradoxical intention. First he is instructed to voice certain phrases, such as "All right, let's go and gouge out eyes! First we'll gouge out the eyes of all patients here in the room, then we'll get the doctors, and in the end the nurses, too. And to gouge out an eye only once is not enough, I'll do it five times to every eye. When I get through with these people here, there will be nobody left here but blind folks. Vitrious [sic] humor will be all over the place. What do we have clean-up women here for? They'll have something to clean up, all right." Or another set of phrases: "Ah, there is a nurse, she's a likely victim for gouging out her eyes. And on the ground floor there are lots of visitors, there is much for me to do. What an opportunity to gouge out eyes *en masse!* And some of them are important people, it pays to go to work on them . . . When I get through with them, nothing is going to be left here but blind people and vitrious [sic] humor. . . ." These phrases are practiced in variations and applied to every one of his compulsive thoughts. In these exercises it was necessary for Dr. Kocourek to get personally involved with the patient because in the beginning the patient showed great resistance to actually practicing paradoxical intention. He was afraid he still might fall victim to an obsessive thought, and besides, he did not really believe in the success of the method. Only after Dr. Kocourek had showed him what to do did the patient agree to cooperate. He repeated the suggested phrases and practiced "a funny way of walking" through the hospital, which, as he later admitted, he actually enjoyed. After these preliminary exercises he was sent to his room and asked to keep on practicing paradoxical intention. In the afternoon of that day the first shy smile crossed his lips, and he remarked: "For the first time I see that my thoughts are really silly!" On day 20 the patient states that he is now able to apply the method without trouble. He is instructed to practice paradoxical intention from now on not only when meeting someone whose eyes he thinks he has gouged out, but to forestall his obsessive thought by thinking about it ahead of time. During the following days he practices paradoxical intention, alone and also with the help of Dr. Ko-courek. The area in which he practices is extended to the children of the nose-ear-and-throat clinic. The patient is encouraged to go to that clinic on some excuse, and to intend paradoxically: "All right, now I'll go and make a few children blind, it's high time that I fill my daily quota. Vitrious [sic] humor will stick to my hands, but I don't give a damn, especially about my obsessive thought." Or: "I've got to have a lot of obsessive thoughts. They'll give me a chance to practice paradoxical intention so I am well prepared when I can go home again." Day 25: The patient informs Dr. Kocourek that he has hardly any obsessive thoughts within the hospital, neither in the presence of adults nor with children. Occasionally he even forgets about paradoxical intention. When he does have an obsessive thought, it doesn't seem to scare him any more. His obsessive thought that everything is not real is also being attacked with paradoxical intention. He practices such phrases as "Okay, so I live in an unreal world. The table here is not real, the doctors are not really here either, but even so, this 'unreal world' is not a bad place to live in. By the way, my thinking about all this proves that I really am here. If I were not real I could not think about it." On the 28th day the patient is allowed for the first time to leave the hospital. He is frightened and does not think he can use the phrases outside. He is advised to formulate his thinking in this manner: "So I'll go out now and cause disaster in the streets. For a change I'll do my gouging out of eyes outside the hospital. I'll get every one of these people, not one will escape me." He leaves the hospital with great misgivings. Upon return he reports happily that he was successful. Despite his apprehensions he was able to use the phrases as learned. Unlike his experiences within the hospital, he did have obsessive thoughts on the street but they didn't scare him. During a walk of one hour he had to turn around only twice. In these cases he had thought of using paradoxical intention too late. "I hardly have obsessive thoughts, but if I do they don't bother me," he reports on day 32. On day 35 the patient is sent home and continues his treatment through visits to the hospital. He participates in group therapy. His condition at the time of his dismissal from the hospital: Inside the hospital he has no more obsessive thoughts; he still has some during his walks on the street but he has learned to formulate his own phrases to deal with them. They are no longer an impediment in his daily routine. The patient immediately finds work, which he accepts. During the first 2 weeks Herr H. visits Dr. Kocourek every day to report on his work and to receive advice as to how to handle himself. After that his visits are reduced to three times a week, and after 4 months once a week. He visits his group therapy only irregularly. The patient is well adjusted to his job. (His boss is satisfied with his performance.) He was able to practice paradoxical intention every day. During working hours he hardly noticed any obsessive thoughts; they only turned up when he was overly tired. During the fifth month of his treatment, shortly before Easter, he developed anxiety about Good Friday. He was afraid he might eat meat on that day without knowing it. He discussed the impending situation with Dr. Kocourek, and they agreed on the following phrasing: "I am going to gulp down a lot of soup, with meat in it. I can't see it but, being an obsessive neurotic, I am sure it's there. For me, eating such a soup is no sin but therapy to get cured." The next week he reports that he had no trouble during the Easter week. He didn't even need the paradoxical intention. In the sixth month of the treatment he suffered a relapse. Obsessive thoughts returned, and paradoxical intention is practiced again. Two weeks later the patient has regained his self-control and is free of obsessive thoughts. He does have occasional relapses which, however, can be straightened out in a few therapy sessions. The patient is advised to immediately see Dr. Kocourek when he fears a turn for the worse. During the seventh month the patient claims his obsessive thoughts have vanished in thin air, and only show up when he is under pressure or physically exhausted. For one weekend he gets a job as tourist guide—an assignment he loves. After the trip—the first outside of Vienna in years—he reports that it was a great success. "I can now master every situation," he declares, "my thoughts no longer bother me." At the end of the seventh month he goes on a vacation with his family, which he can spend without any trouble. After that he doesn't show up to see Dr. Kocourek for 3 months. As he explained later, he felt well and did not need any doctor. He felt no need to use paradoxical intention during that time. For 3 months he had been free of obsessive thoughts. "That had never happened before," he declared. Although obsessive thoughts sometimes recur, he no longer feels compelled to actions. He also learned to react to occurring obsessive thoughts with equanimity. They no longer interfere with his daily life. The success of the treatment can be seen from the fact that Herr H. was able to work the entire 14 months since his release from the hospital and did not change jobs.

Results obtained by paradoxical intention in obsessive-compulsive neurosis must be evaluated with a view to the fact that here "the prognosis is probably worse than that of any other neurotic disorder" (Solyom *et al.*, 1972): "A recent summary of 12 follow-up studies on obsessive neurosis from seven different countries sets a nonimproved rate of 50% (Yates, 1970)." Eight studies on the behavioral treatment of obsessive neurosis reported that only "46% of the published cases were rated improved" (Solyom *et al.*, 1972).

Last but not least, it has long been observed that the paradoxical intention technique lends itself to the treatment of sleeplessness. As an example, I would like to quote another case, in which Sadiq used the technique with a fifty-four-year-old woman who had become addicted to sleeping pills. One night she came out of her room about 10 P.M., and the following dialogue ensued:

Patient: Can I have my sleeping pill?
Therapist: I am sorry I can't give you the pill tonight as we ran out of it and forgot to get a fresh supply in the evening.

P.: Oh, how would I go to sleep now?

T.: Well, I guess you have to try it without the pill tonight. [She went into her room, kept lying on her bed for about 2 hours and came out again.]

P.: I just can't sleep.

T.: Well, then why don't you go to your room, lie down, and try not to sleep. Let's see if you cannot stay awake all night.

P.: I thought I am crazy, but it looks like you are too.

T.: It is fun to be crazy for a while. Isn't it?

P.: You really meant that?

T.: What?

P.: Trying not to go to sleep.

T.: Of course, I meant that. Go try it. Let us see if you can keep awake all night. And I will help by calling you every time I make a round. How about that?

P.: O.K.

"In the morning," Sadiq concludes, "when I went to wake her up for the breakfast, she was still asleep." What comes to mind in this context is the following episode, reported by Jay Haley (1963): "During a lecture on hypnosis a young man said to Milton H. Erickson, 'You may be able to hypnotize other people, but you can't hypnotize me!' Dr. Erickson invited the subject to the demonstration platform, asked him to sit down, and then said to him, 'I want you to stay awake, wider and wider awake, wider and wider awake.' The subject promptly went into a deep trance."

Although insomnia yields to paradoxical intention, the insomniac patient may hesitate to apply it if he is not cognizant of a well-established fact, that is, that the body provides itself with the minimum amount of sleep it really needs, by itself. So the patient need not worry and may as well start using paradoxical intention, in other words, wishing—for a change—for a sleepless night.

Medlicott (1969) used paradoxical intention to influence not only the patient's sleep but also his dreams. He applied the technique especially in phobic cases and found it extremely helpful even to an analytically oriented psychiatrist, he reported. What is most remarkable, however, is "the attempted application of the principle to nightmares along the lines apparently used by the African tribe and reported some years back in *Transcultural Psychiatry*. The patient had made excellent progress in hospital, where she was sent because of a severe neurotic depressive state. Encouraging her to practice paradoxical intention had resulted in her being able to go back home, take over responsibilities, and meet her conscious anxieties quite effectively. However, some time later she returned, complaining that her sleep was disturbed by dreams in which she was pursued by persons who were going to shoot her or knife her. Her husband's sleep was disturbed by her screaming and he would wake her. She was firmly instructed to try and dream further such dreams, but stand and be shot or knifed, and her husband was instructed that under no circumstances was he to wake her if she screamed. The next time I saw her she told he there had been no more nightmares, although her husband complained that he was wakened by her laughing in her sleep."

There are a few instances in which paradoxical intention has been tried even with psychotic manifestations such as auditory hallucinations. The following is again a quotation from the paper by Sadiq:

Frederick was a 24-year-old patient suffering from schizophrenia. The predominant symptomatology was auditory hallucinations. He heard voices making fun of him, and he felt threatened by them. He was in the hospital for 10 days when I talked to him. Fred came out of his room around two o'clock in the morning and complained that he was not able to sleep because the voices wouldn't let him.

Patient: I cannot sleep. Could you please give me some sleeping pills?

Therapist: Why can't you sleep? Is something bothering you?

P.: Yes, I hear these voices making fun of me and I just can't get rid of them.

T.: Well, did you talk about these to your doctor?

P.: He asked me not to pay any attention to them. But I just can't do it.

T.: Did you try not paying attention to them?

P.: I have been trying all these days, but it just doesn't seem to work.

T.: How would you like to do something different?

P.: What do you mean?

T.: Go, lie down on your bed and pay all the attention you can to these voices. Don't let them stop. Try to hear more and more.

P.: You are kidding.

T.: I am not. Why not try to enjoy these God damn things.

P.: But my doctor . . .

T.: Why don't you give it a try?

So he decided to give it a try, I checked him after about 45 minutes, and he was sound asleep. In the morning, I asked him how did he sleep last night. "Oh, I slept alright," was the answer. I asked him if he did hear voices for long, and he said, "I don't know, I think I fell asleep soon."

This case is somewhat reminiscent of what Huber (1968), having visited a Zen psychiatric hospital, described in terms of "emphasis on living with the suffering rather than complaining about it, analyzing, or trying to avoid it." In this context, he mentions the case of a Buddhist nun who had become acutely disturbed:

> The major symptom was her terror at the snakes she saw crawling over her body. Physicians and then psychologists and psychiatrists were brought to see her but they could do nothing for her. Finally a Zen psychiatrist was brought in. He was in her room for only 5 minutes. "What is the trouble?" he asked. "The snakes crawl over my body and frighten me." The Zen psychiatrist thought a bit and then said, "I must leave now, but I shall come back to see you in a week. While I am gone, I want you to observe the snakes very carefully so that when I return you will be able to describe their movements accurately to me." In 7 days he returned and found the nun doing her duties she had been assigned before her illness. He greeted her and then asked, "Did you follow my instructions?" "Indeed," she answered, "I centered all my attention on the snakes. But alas, I saw them no more, for when I observed them carefully they were gone."

If the principle of paradoxical intention is of any worth, it would be strange and improbable if it had not been discovered long ago, and rediscovered again and again. Logotherapy had to make it into a scientifically acceptable methodology. As to methodology, however, it should be noted that among the authors who have applied paradoxical intention with much success and afterward published on their experience with the technique, many had never had any formal training in logotherapy nor ever watched a logotherapist in action, even in the setting of classroom demonstrations. They have learned solely from the literature in the field. That even lay people can benefit from a book on logotherapy by way of self-administered paradoxical intention may be seen from the following excerpt, quoted from another unsolicited letter:

For five months I have been searching for information concerning paradoxical intention here in Chicago. I first learned of your method through your book *The Doctor and the Soul*. Since then I have made many phone calls to different places. I ran an ad ("Would like to hear from anyone having knowledge of or treated by paradoxical intention for agoraphobia . . .") in our Chicago *Tribune* for a week but received no replies. So why am I still trying to find out more about paradoxical intention? Because during this time, I have used paradoxical intention on my own, following as best I could from examples in the book. I have had agoraphobia for 14 years. I had a nervous breakdown at 24 while going to a Freudian psychiatrist for 3 years for a different problem. In the third year I broke down. I could no longer work, or even go outside. My sister had to support me as best as she could. After 4 years of trying to help myself, I put myself into a state hospital—my weight had dropped to 84 pounds. Six weeks later I was released "improved" from the hospital. Several months later I had a breakdown again. I could not leave the house at all. This time I went to a hypnotist for 2 years. It wasn't too much help. I had panics, tremors, felt faint. I feared getting the panics, and I always got the panics. I'm afraid of big stores, crowds, distances, etc. Nothing has really changed in 14 years. A few weeks ago, I started to feel nervous and frightened, when your method came to mind. I said to myself, "I'll show everyone in the street how well I can panic and collapse." I seemed to quiet down. I continued to a small nearby store. While having my items checked out, I again felt nervous and started to feel panicky. I noticed my hands were sweating. Not wanting to run out just as the man was almost through, I used paradoxical intention, saying to myself, "I'll show this man how much I can really sweat. He'll be so amazed." It wasn't until I got my groceries and was on my way home that I realized I had stopped being nervous and frightened. Two weeks ago our neighborhood carnival started. I was always so nervous and scared. This time before I left the house I thought to myself, "I will try to panic and collapse." For the first time I went right in the middle of the carnival where the crowd was. Yes, at times the fear thoughts would start and I started to feel the panic coming on, but each time I used paradoxical intention. Whenever I felt uncomfortable, I used your method. I stayed 3 hours and hadn't enjoyed myself so much in years. I felt pride for the first time in a long time. Since then I have done many things that I would not have done before. No, I am not cured, nor have I done many of the bigger things that I can't do. But I know something is different when I'm out. There are times I feel as though I had never been ill. Using paradoxical intention makes me feel stronger. For the first time I feel I have something to fight back with, against the panics. I don't feel so helpless against them. I have tried many methods, but none gave me the quick relief your method did, even if they aren't the most difficult things I do. I believe in your method, because I have tried it on my own with just a book. Sincerely . . . P.S. I also use paradoxical intention for sleepless nights, and it puts me to sleep in a short time. A few of my friends also use it successfully.

Incidentally, the patient also reported "an experiment" she had tried:

When I went to bed I was visualizing myself in situations that make me panic. What I wanted to do was practice paradoxical intention at home, so I'd be good at it when I'm out. Well, in the past (before using paradoxical intention) I would try to remain calm as I went through this visualization and would become upset seeing myself in these situations. Now (when I try to panic in my visualization so I can use paradoxical intention) I'm not afraid, I don't panic. I guess because I want to panic I can't.

Another case of self-administered paradoxical intention is the following:

On Thursday morning, I awoke out of my sleep, disturbed, thinking, "I'll never get well, what am I going to do?" Well, I was getting more and more depressed as the day went on. I could feel the tears starting to come. I was feeling so hopeless. All of a sudden, I thought of trying paradoxical intention on this depression. I said to myself, "I'll see how depressed I can get." I thought to myself, "I'll really get depressed and start crying, I'll cry all over the place." In my mind, I started to imagine great big tears rolling down my cheeks, and I continued to imagine that I was crying so much that I flooded the house. At this thought and sight in my mind, I started laughing. I imagined my sister coming home and saying, "Esther, what the hell have you been doing, did you have to cry so much that you flooded the house?" Well, Dr. Frankl, at the thought of this whole scene I began laughing and laughing, so much so that I became frightened that I was laughing so much. I then said to myself, "I'll laugh so much and so loud that all the neighbors will run over to see who's laughing so much." This seemed to tone me down a bit. That was Thursday morning, today is Saturday and the depression is still gone. I guess using paradoxical intention that day was like trying to watch yourself in a mirror when you're crying— for some reason it makes you stop. I cannot cry

while looking into a mirror. P.S. I did not write this
letter for help, because I helped myself.

That people can "help themselves" by using paradoxical intention on themselves is conceivable only if
this technique is understood as utilizing, or mobilizing,
a coping mechanism wired into each and every human
being. That is why paradoxical intention is often applied unwittingly. Ruven A. K. reported the following:

> I was looking forward to serving in the Israeli
> army. I found meaning in my country's struggle for
> survival. Therefore, I decided to serve in the best
> way I could. I volunteered to the top troops in the
> army, the paratroopers. I was exposed to situations
> where my life was in danger. For example, jumping
> out of the plane for the first time. I experienced fear
> and was literally shaking and trying to hide this fact
> made me shake more intensely. Then I decided to let
> my fear show and shake as much as I could, and after
> a while the shaking and trembling stopped. Uninten-
> tionally I was using paradoxical intention, and sur-
> prisingly enough it worked.

In an opposite instance the principle underlying
paradoxical intention was used not only unwittingly
but also unwillingly. This story concerns a client of my
former student Uriel Meshoulam of Harvard University, who reported it to me as follows:

> The patient was called to the Australian army, and
> was sure he would avoid the draft because of his
> stuttering. To make a long story short, he tried three
> times to demonstrate his speech difficulty to the
> doctor, but could not. Ironically, he was released on
> grounds of high blood pressure. The Australian army

probably does not believe him until today, that he is a stutterer.*

Just as individuals can use paradoxical intention inadvertently, so can whole groups. Not only Zen psychiatry but also other forms of "ethnopsychiatry seem to apply principles that later on have been systematized by logotherapy," as was pointed out by Ochs (1968). Thus, "the principle underlying the therapy of the Ifaluk is logotherapeutic," and the Shaman of Mexican-American folk psychiatry, "the Curandero, is a logotherapist. Wallace and Vogelson point out the fact that ethnopsychiatric systems often use psychotherapeutic principles which only recently have been recognized by Western psychiatric systems. It appears that logotherapy is one nexus between the two. . . ." (Ochs, 1969).

---

* What in this context comes to mind is a case from the files of Dr. Elisabeth Lukas as published in *Uniquest* (7, 1977, pp. 32–33): "Anneliese K., 54, married, no children, suffering from heavy depression which has been treated psychopharmacologically. Nevertheless, she remained fearful of relapses. The logotherapeutic method of paradoxical intention is used to show her how to handle her fears. She is instructed to distance herself from her phobia, to use her sense of humor. She is instructed to use the following formulations when she expects anticipatory anxiety: 'Now, the time has come again for one of my nice little depressions. I haven't had one in ages, maybe today around lunch, that would be a good time, to take away my appetite.' Or: 'OK, you depression, just try to get me, and get me good, but today you won't get me.' Or: 'I don't know what's the matter with me, I can't get depressed any more, and I was so good at it before. I must be out of practice. Everything seems bright and cheerful, and it ought to be sad and gray, and I should be in deep despair.' For the past half year Frau K. had no relapses and has to use paradoxical intention less and less often."

Similar claims have been made with respect to Morita psychotherapy, another Eastern method. As was evidenced by Yamamoto (1968) and Noonan (1969), Morita therapy possesses "a remarkable number of similarities to Frankl's paradoxical intention," and according to Reynolds (1976) the two methods employ "quite similar therapeutic tactics discovered independently thousands of miles apart." But, as Noonan (1969) notes, whereas Morita therapy reflects the Eastern world view, the Western view underlies logotherapy. Reynolds concludes: "Frankl represents a culture in which individualism is supreme and rationalism requires the discovery of personal goals," while "Morita represents a group-oriented culture in which tradition laid out the goals as givens."

Thus logotherapy has been anticipated, although not systematically, by people and peoples all along. By the same token, however, logotherapy has anticipated much that is being rediscovered, more or less methodically, by behavior therapists, In short, logotherapy has been anticipated by the past, and itself has "anticipated the future, which has in the last decade caught up with logotherapy: (Steinzor, 1969). For example, according to logotherapy, "fear of fear" arises from the patient's apprehensions about the potential effects of his fear (Frankl, 1953). An experiment conducted by Valins and Ray (quoted from Marks, 1969) confirms this logotherapeutic hypothesis: "Students with snake phobias were given false auditory feedback of their heart sounds while watching slides of snakes. They were led to believe that their heart rate did not increase on seeing the snakes. This procedure led to significantly decreased avoidance of snakes."

Logotherapy also teaches that "fear of fear" induces "flight from fear," and that a phobia really starts when this pathogenic pattern of avoidance has been established. Paradoxical intention then obviates such avoidance by generating a total inversion of the patient's intention to flee from his fear (Frankl, 1953). This is in perfect accordance with the finding of Marks (1970) that "the phobia can be properly overcome only when the patient faces the phobic situation again." The same principle also is implemented by behavioristically oriented techniques such as "flooding." As Rachman, Hodgson and Marks (1971) explain it, during flooding treatment the patient is "encouraged and persuaded to enter the most disturbing situation." Similarly, in the behavioristically oriented treatment called "prolonged exposure," discussed in a paper by Watson, Gaind and Marks (1971), the patient is "encouraged to approach the feared object as closely and as quickly as he can, and avoidance is discouraged." Marks (1969) recognizes expressly that flooding "has certain similarities to the paradoxical intention technique." Marks (1974) also noted that the paradoxical intention technique "closely resembles that now termed modeling" (Bandura, 1968). Likewise, similarities to paradoxical intention can be discovered in the techniques called "anxiety provoking," "exposure *in vivo*," "implosion," "induced anxiety," "modification of expectations" and "prolonged exposure"—i.e., in techniques on which the first material was published between 1967 and 1971.

DEREFLECTION

Of the three pathogenic patterns that are distinguished by logotherapy, so far two have been discussed: the phobic pattern, characterized by flight from fear, and the obsessive-compulsive pattern, which is distinguished by the fight against obsessions and compulsions. What then is the third pattern? It is the sexual neurotic pattern, which again is characterized by the patient's fight. Here, however, the patient is not fighting *against* anything, but rather *for* sexual pleasure. But it is a tenet of logotherapy that the more one aims at pleasure the more he misses it.

Whenever potency and orgasm are made a target of intention they are also made a target of attention (Frankl, 1952). In logotherapy the terms we use are "hyper-intention" and "hyper-reflection" (Frankl, 1962). The two phenomena reinforce each other so that a feedback mechanism is established. In order to secure potency and orgasm, the patient pays attention to himself, to his own performance and experience. To the same extent, attention is withdrawn from the partner and whatever the partner has to offer in terms of stimuli that might arouse the patient sexually. As a consequence, potency and orgasm are in fact diminished. This in turn enhances the patient's hyper-intention and the vicious circle is completed.

If this circle is to be broken, centrifugal forces have to be brought into play. Instead of striving for potency and orgasm, the patient should be himself, give himself. Instead of observing and watching himself, he should forget himself. In order to implement this pro-

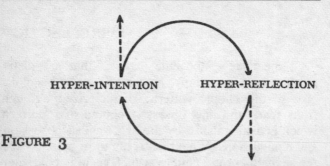

FIGURE 3

cess—in other words, in order to counteract the patient's hyper-reflection—another logotherapeutic technique has been developed: "de-reflection" (Frankl, 1955).

Kaczanowski (1965, 1967) has contributed illustrative case reports regarding de-reflection and, more specifically, the logotherapeutic treatment of impotence. Here let me just quote a case of impotence in which Kaczanowski's patient is said to have been "the lucky one to get the most glamorous girl of his acquaintance as his wife" and understandably "wanted to give her the greatest possible sexual pleasure, which she deserved and certainly expected." Kaczanowski reasoned that the patient's "desperate striving for sexual perfection and his hyper-intention of virility could be the reason for his impotence." He succeeded in helping the patient "to see that real love had many aspects worthy of cultivation. The patient learned that if he loved his wife he could *give* her *himself,* instead of trying to give her a sexual climax. Then her pleasure would be the consequence of his attitude, not an aim in itself" (Kaczanowski, 1967).

What is more important, in addition to counteracting the patient's self-defeating "fight for pleasure," Kaczanowski enacted de-reflection perfectly along the lines I described first in 1946 in German and in 1952 in English: Kaczanowski "told the patient and his wife that no attempt at intercourse should be made for an undetermined period of time. This instruction relieved the patient's anticipatory anxiety. A few weeks later, the patient broke the order; the wife tried to remind him but, fortunately, she disregarded it too. Since that time, their sexual relations have been normal" (Kaczanowski, 1967). One is tempted to add: and they lived happily thereafter for years.

In my publications describing this technique I have also pointed out that in the formation of hyper-intention a decisive factor is a "demand quality" that the patient attaches to sexual intercourse. This demand quality may be engendered by (1) the situation, "which appears to be one of *Hic Rhodus, hic salta*" (Frankl, 1952); (2) the patient (his fight for pleasure); or (3) the partner. In cases falling under the third category, the patient is potent only as long as he can take the initiative.

Recently two more pathogenic factors have entered the etiology of impotence: (4) peer pressures and (5) pressure groups. Here the demand quality emanates from a society that is preoccupied with achievement and extends that emphasis to sexual performance.

Ginsberg, Frosch & Shapiro (1972) have pointed to the "increased sexual freedom of women" and its result that "these newly free women *demanded* sexual performance." Likewise, Stewart (1972), reporting on impotence at Oxford in the medical magazine *Pulse*, notes that "females run around *demanding* sexual rights." Small wonder that "young men now appear more frequently with complaints of impotence," as Ginsberg, Frosch and Shapiro conclude. These observations, in full accordance with many other observations on various continents, seem to corroborate on a mass scale the logotherapeutic hypothesis on the etiology of impotence. As to group pressures, just consider pornography and sex education, both of which have become big industry. "The hidden persuaders" are at their service, and so are the mass media, fostering a climate of sexual expectation and demand.

To illustrate the logotherapeutic approach to sexual neurosis, let me quote from the first pertinent publication in English. The following "trick was devised to remove the demand placed on the patient by his partner. We advise the patient to inform his partner that he consulted a doctor about his difficulty, who said that his case was not serious, and the prognosis favorable. Most important, however, is that he tell his partner that the doctor also has absolutely forbidden coitus. His partner now expects no sexual activity and the patient is 'released.' Through this release from the demands of his partner it is possible for his sexuality to be expressed again, undisturbed and unblocked by the feeling that something is demanded or expected from him. Often, in fact, his partner is not only surprised when the potency of the man becomes apparent, but she goes so far as to reject him because of the doctor's orders. When the patient has no other goal before him than a mutual sexual play of tenderness, then, and then only, in the process of such play is the vicious circle broken" (Frankl, 1952).

As Sahakian and Sahakian (1972) as well as other authors remark, the technique outlined above, which I first published in German in 1946, has been paralleled in 1970 by Masters and Johnson in their research on human sexual inadequacy. In view of the importance that logotherapy ascribes to both anticipatory anxiety and hyper-reflection as pathogenic factors in the etiology of sexual neuroses, one may question the contention of Masters and Johnson (1976) that "neither fears of sexual performance nor the closely related spectator role has been sufficiently recognized as a primary deterrent to effective sexual functioning."

The technique I published in 1946 is illustrated by the following case report, which I owe to my former student at U.S. International University, Myron J. Horn:

> A young couple came in complaining of incompatibility. The wife had told the husband often that he was a lousy lover, and that she was going to start having affairs to satisfy herself. I asked them to spend at least one hour in bed together nude every evening for the next week. I said it was okay to neck a little but under no circumstances were they to have intercourse. When they returned the following week they said they tried not to have sex but had had intercourse three times. Acting irate, I demanded they try again next week to follow my instructions. Midweek, they called and said they were unable to comply and were having relations several times a day. They did not return. A year later I met the mother of the girl, who relayed that the couple had not had a recurrence of the impotence problem.

The art of improvisation plays a decisive role in the logotherapeutic treatment of impotence. I am indebted to Joseph B. Fabry for a case history from which both the possibility and necessity of improvisation can be seen:

> After I had been lecturing about dereflection, one of the participants asked if she could apply the technique to her boyfriend. He found himself impotent, first with a girl with whom he had had a brief affair, and now with Susan. Using a Frankl technique, we decided that Susan should tell her friend that she was under the care of a doctor who had given her some medication and told her not to have intercourse for a month. They were allowed to be physically close and do everything up to actual intercourse. Next week Susan reported that it had worked. Her friend was a psychologist who had taken Masters and Johnson instruction in curing sex failures, and was advising his own patients in such matters. Four weeks later Susan reported that he had had a relapse but that she had "cured" him on her own initiative. Since she could not have repeated the story about doctor's orders, she had told her friend that she had seldom if ever reached orgasm and asked him not to have intercourse that night but to help her with her problem of orgasm. Again it worked. By her inventiveness Susan has shown that she indeed understood well the workings of dereflection. . . . Since then no more problem with impotence had occurred.

The "centrifugal forces," as I put it at the outset, were brought into play by Susan ingeniously. In order to assist her boyfriend in overcoming hyper-intention as well as hyper-reflection, in order to help him in giving himself and forgetting himself, she took on the role of a patient. He was allotted the role of a therapist.

The report from which I am now going to quote concerns a patient of mine suffering from frigidity rather than impotence. I published a sketch of it in 1962:

> The patient, a young woman, came to me complaining of being frigid. The case history showed that in her childhood she had been sexually abused by her father. However, it was not this traumatic experience in itself that had eventuated in her sexual neurosis. It turned out that, as a result of reading popular psychoanalytic literature, the patient lived all the time in fearful expectation of the toll that her traumatic experience would someday take. This anticipatory anxiety resulted in both excessive intention to confirm her femininity and excessive attention centered upon herself rather than upon her partner. This was enough to incapacitate the patient for the peak experience of sexual pleasure, since the orgasm was made an object of intention and an object of attention as well. Although I knew that short-term logotherapy would do, I deliberately told her that she had to be put on a waiting list for a couple of months. For the time being, however, she should no longer be concerned about whether or not she was capable of orgasm, but should concentrate on her partner, better to say whatever made him loveable in her eyes. "Just promise me that you won't give a damn for orgasm," I asked her. "This we'll take up discussing only after a couple of months, when I start treating you." What I had anticipated happened after a couple of days, not to say nights. She returned to report that, for the first time not caring for orgasm, she had experienced it the first time.

Darrell Burnett reported a parallel case: "A woman suffering from frigidity kept observing what was going on in her body during intercourse, trying to do everything according to the manuals. She was told to switch her attention to her husband. A week later she experienced an orgasm."

Now, I would like to quote from an unpublished report on a case of premature ejaculation treated by Gustave Ehrentraut, who studied logotherapy at U.S. International University. He did not apply dereflection but rather paradoxical intention:

> Over the past sixteen years Fred's ability to prolong the sexual union had continually decreased. I attempted to deal with the problem through a combination of behavior modification, bioenergetics and sexual education. He had been in sessions for a period of two months and no significant change had been accomplished. I decided to attempt Frankl's paradoxical intention. I informed Fred that he was not to worry about his premature ejaculation, that he wasn't going to be able to change it anyway, and that he should therefore attempt only to satisfy himself. He should cut the duration of intercourse to one minute. The next session, seven days later, Fred related that he had intercourse twice that week, and he could not reach a climax in less than five minutes. I told him that he must reduce the time. The next week he was up to seven minutes the first time and eleven minutes the second time. Denise stated that she had been satisfied both times. Since that visit they have not felt it necessary to return.

Claude Farris is a California counselor who once treated another type of sexual neurosis and like Gustave Ehrentraut, he used paradoxical intention:

> Mr. and Mrs. Y. were referred to me by Mrs. Y.'s gynecologist. Mrs. Y. was experiencing pain during

intercourse. Mr. and Mrs. Y. had been married for three years and indicated that this had been a problem from the beginning of their marriage. Mrs. Y. had been raised in a Catholic convent by sisters, and sex was a taboo subject. I then instructed her in paradoxical intention. She was instructed not to try to relax her genital area but to actually tighten it as tight as possible and to try to make it impossible for her husband to penetrate her and he was instructed to try as hard as he could to get in. They returned after one week and reported that they had followed instructions and had enjoyed painless intercourse for the very first time. Three more weekly sessions indicated no return of the symptoms. Paradoxical intention has proved effective in many cases in my experience, and at times almost works me out of business.

What I regard as most remarkable about Farris's inventive tackling of the case is the idea of bringing about relaxation through paradoxical intention. What comes to mind in this context is an experiment that David L. Norris, a California researcher, once conducted. In this setting, Steve S., the subject, "was actively trying to relax. The electromyograph meter which I use in my research read constantly at a high level (50 micro-amperes) until I told him that he probably would never be able to learn to relax and should resign himself to the fact that he would always be tense. A few minutes later Steve S. stated, 'Oh hell, I give up,' at which time the meter reading immediately dropped to a low level (10 micro-amperes), with such speed that I thought the unit had become disconnected. For the succeeding sessions Steve S. was successful because he was *not* trying to relax."

Edith Weisskopf-Joelson has reported something similar: "I was recently trained in doing Transcendental Meditation but I gave it up after a few weeks because I feel I meditate spontaneously on my own, but when I start meditating formally I actually stop meditating."

Videant consules and counselors.

REFERENCES

Agras, W. S. (ed.), *Behavior Modification: Principles and Clinical Applications*. Boston, Little, Brown and Company, 1972.

Allport, G. W., Preface, in V. E. Frankl, *From Death-Camp to Existentialism*. Boston, Beacon Press, 1959.

———, *Personality and Social Encounter*. Boston, Beacon Press, 1960.

Bandura, A., "Modelling Approaches to the Modification of Phobic Disorders," in *The Role of Learning in Psychotherapy*. London, Churchill, 1968.

Benedikt, F. M., *Zur Therapie angst- und zwangsneurotischer Symptome mit Hilfe der "Paradoxen Intention" und "Dereflexion" nach V. E. Frankl*. Dissertation, University of Munich, 1968.

Briggs, G. J. F., "Courage and Identity." Paper read before the Royal Society of Medicine, London, April 5, 1970.

Buhler, C., and M. Allen, *Introduction to Humanistic Psychology*. Monterey, Brooks-Cole, 1972.

Dilling, H., H. Rosefeldt, G. Kockott, and H. Heyse, "*Verhaltenstherapie bei Phobien, Zwangsneurosen, sexuellen Störungen und Süchten*." Fortschr. Neurol. Psychiat. 39, 1971, 293–344.

Frankl, V. E., "*Zur geistigen Problematik der Psychotherapie*." Zentralblatt für Psychotherapie, 10, 1938, 33.

———, "*Zur medikamentösen Unterstützung der Psychotherapie bei Neurosen*." Schweizer Archiv für Neurologie und Psychiatrie, 43, 1939, 26–31.

———, *Ärztliche Seelsorge*. Vienna, Deuticke, 1946.

———, *Die Psychotherapie in der Praxis*. Vienna, Deuticke, 1947.

———, "The Pleasure Principle and Sexual Neurosis." *International Journal of Sexology*, 5, 1952, 128–30.

————, "Angst und Zwang." *Acta Psychotherapeutica*, 1, 1953, 111–20.

————, *The Doctor and the Soul: From Psychotherapy to Logotherapy*. New York, Knopf, 1955.

————, *Theorie und Therapie der Neurosen*. Vienna, Urban & Schwarzenberg, 1956.

————, "On Logotherapy and Existential Analysis." *American Journal of Psychoanalysis*, 18, 1958, 28–37.

————, "Beyond Self-Actualization and Self-Expression." Paper read before the Conference on Existential Psychiatry, Chicago, December 13, 1959.

————, "Paradoxical Intention: A Logotherapeutic Technique." *American Journal of Psychotherapy*, 14, 1960, 520–35.

————, *Man's Search for Meaning: An Introduction to Logotherapy*. Boston, Beacon Press, 1962.

————, "Logotherapy and Existential Analysis: A review." *American Journal of Psychotherapy*, 20, 1966, 252–60.

————, *Psychotherapy and Existentialism: Selected papers on Logotherapy*. New York, Washington Square Press, 1967.

————, *The Will to Meaning: Foundations and Applications of Logotherapy*. New York, New American Library, 1969.

Gerz, H. O., "The Treatment of the Phobic and the Obsessive-Compulsive Patient Using Paradoxical Intention sec. Viktor E. Frankl." *Journal of Neuropsychiatry*, 3, 6, 1962, 375–87.

————, "Experience with the Logotherapeutic Technique of Paradoxical Intention in the Treatment of Phobic and Obsessive-Compulsive Patients." *American Journal of Psychiatry*, 123, 5, 1966, 548–53.

Ginsberg, G. L., W. A. Frosch, and T. Shapiro, "The New Impotence." *Arch. Gen. Psychiat.*, 26, 1972, 218–20.

Hand, I., Y. Lamontagne, and I. M. Marks, "Group Exposure (Flooding) *in vivo* for Agoraphobics." *Brit. J. Psychiat.*, 124, 1974, 588–602.

Havens, L. L., "Paradoxical intention." *Psychiatry & Social Science Review*, 2, 2, 1968, 16–19.

Henkel, D., C. Schmook, and R. Bastine, *Praxis der Psychotherapie*, 17, 1972, 236.

Huber, J., *Through an Eastern Window*. New York: Bantam Books, 1968.

Jacobs, M., "An Holistic Approach to Behavior Therapy." In A. A. Lazarus (ed.), *Clinical Behavior Therapy*. New York, Brunner-Mazel, 1972.

Kaczanowski, G., in A. Burton (ed.), *Modern Psychotherapeutic Practice*. Palo Alto, Science and Behavior, 1965.

————, "Logotherapy: A New Psychotherapeutic Tool." *Psychosomatics*, 8, 1967, 158–61.

Kocourek, K., E. Niebauer, and P. Polak, *"Ergebnisse der klinischen Anwendung der Logotherapie."* In V. E. Frankl, V. E. von Gebsattel and J. H. Schultz (eds.), *Handbuch der Neurosenlehre und Psychotherapie*. Munich, Urban & Schwarzenberg, 1959.

Kvilhaug, B., *"Klinische Erfahrungen mit der logotherapeutischen Technik der Paradoxen Intention."* Paper read before the Austrian Medical Society of Psychotherapy, Vienna, July 18, 1963.

Lapinsohn, L. I., "Relationship of the Logotherapeutic Concepts of Anticipatory Anxiety and Paradoxical Intention to the Neurophysiological Theory of Induction." *Behav. neuropsychiat.*, 3, 3–4, 1971, 12–24.

Lazarus, A. A., *Behavior Therapy and Beyond*. New York, McGraw-Hill, 1971.

Lehembre, J., *"L'intention paradoxale, procédé de psychothérapie."* *Acta Neurologica et Psychiatrica Belgica*, 64, 1964, 725–35.

Leslie, R. C., *Jesus and Logotherapy: The Ministry of Jesus as Interpreted through the Psychotherapy of Viktor Frankl*. New York, Abingdon, 1965.

Lorenz, K., *On Aggression*. New York, Bantam, 1967.

Lyons, J., "Existential Psychotherapy." *Journal of Abnormal and Social Psychology*, 62, 1961, 242–49.

Marks, I. M., *Fears and Phobias*. New York, Academic Press, 1969.

————, "The Origin of Phobic States." *American Journal of Psychotherapy*, 24, 1970, 652–76.

————, "Paradoxical Intention." In W. S. Agras (ed.), *Behavior Modification*. Boston: Little, Brown and Company, 1972.

————, "Treatment of Obsessive-Compulsive Disorders." In H. H. Strupp *et al.* (eds.), *Psychotherapy and Behavior Change 1973*. Chicago, Aldine, 1974.

Masters, W. H., and V. E. Johnson, "Principles of the New Sex Therapy." *Am. J. Psychiatry*, 133, 1976, 548–54.

Medlicott, R. W., "The Management of Anxiety." *New Zealand Medical Journal,* 70, 1969, 155–58.

Muller-Hegemann, D., "Methodological Approaches in Psychotherapy." *American Journal of Psychotherapy,* 17, 1963, 554–68.

Noonan, J. Robert, "A Note on an Eastern Counterpart of Frankl's Paradoxical Intention." *Psychologia,* 12, 1969, 147–49.

Ochs, J. M., "Logotherapy and Religious Ethnopsychiatric Therapy." Paper presented to the Pennsylvania Sociological Society at Villanova University, 1968.

Pervin, L. A. "Existentialism, Psychology, and Psychotherapy." *American Psychologist,* 15, 1960, 305–309.

Polak, P., "Frankl's Existential Analysis." *American Journal of Psychotherapy,* 3, 1949, 517–22.

Rachman, S., R. Hodgson, and I. M. Marks. "The Treatment of Chronic Obsessive-Compulsive Neurosis." *Behav. Res. Ther.,* 9, 1971, 237–47.

Raskin, David E., and Zanvel E. Klein, "Losing a Symptom Through Keeping It: A Review of Paradoxical Treatment Techniques and Rationale." *Archives of General Psychiatry,* 33, 1976, 548–55.

Reynolds, D. K., *Morita Psychotherapy.* Berkeley, University of California Press, 1976.

Sahakian, W. S., and B. J. Sahakian, "Logotherapy as a Personality Theory." *Israel Annals of Psychiatry,* 10, 1972, 230–44.

Solyom, L., J. Garza-Perez, B. L. Ledwidge, and C. Solyom, "Paradoxical Intention in the Treatment of Obsessive Thoughts: A Pilot Study." *Comprehensive Psychiatry,* 13, 1972, 3, 291–97.

Spiegelberg, H., *Phenomenology in Psychology and Psychiatry.* Evanston, Northwestern University Press, 1972.

Steinzor, B., in *Psychiatry & Social Science Review,* 3, 1969, 23–28.

Stewart, J. M., in *Psychology and Life Newsletter,* 1, 1, 1972, 5.

Tweedie, D. F., *Logotherapy and the Christian Faith: An Evaluation of Frankl's Existential Approach to Psychotherapy.* Grand Rapids, Baker Book House, 1961.

Ungersma, A. J., *The Search for Meaning.* Philadelphia, Westminster Press, 1961.

Victor, R. G., and C. M. Krug, "Paradoxical Intention in the Treatment of Compulsive Gambling." *American Journal of Psychotherapy,* 21, 1967, 808–14.

Watson, J. P., R. Gaind, and I. M. Marks, "Prolonged Exposure."
Brit. Med. J., 1, 1971, 13–15.

Weisskopf-Joelson, E., "Some Comments on a Viennese School of
Psychiatry." *Journal of Abnormal and Social Psychology*, 51,
1955, 701–703.

———, "The Present Crisis in Psychotherapy." *The Journal of
Psychology*, 69, 1968, 107–15.

Yamamoto, I. *"Die japanische Morita-Therapie im Vergleich zu der
Existenzanalyse und Logotherapie Frankls."* In W. Bitter (ed.),
Abendländische Therapie und östliche Weisheit. Stuttgart, Klett,
1958.

Yates, A. J., *Behavior Therapy*. New York, Wiley, 1970.

NOTE: L. M. Ascher pointed out that "paradoxical
intention was effective even though the expectations
of the clients were assumed to be in opposition to the
functioning of the technique." ("A Review of Literature on the Treatment of Insomnia with Paradoxical
Intention," unpublished paper.)

Logotherapy: An English Language Bibliography

1. BOOKS

BULKA, REUVEN P., *The Quest for Ultimate Meaning: Principles and Applications of Logotherapy*. Foreword by Viktor E. Frankl. New York, Philosophical Library, 1979.

CRUMBAUGH, JAMES C., *Everything to Gain: A Guide to Self-fulfillment Through Logoanalysis*. Preface by Victor E. Frankl. Chicago, Nelson-Hall, 1973.

———, W. M. WOOD, and W. C. WOOD, *Logotherapy: New Help for Problem Drinkers*. Chicago, Nelson-Hall, 1980.

FABRY, JOSEPH B., *The Pursuit of Meaning: Viktor Frankl, Logotherapy, and Life*. Preface by Viktor E. Frankl. Boston, Beacon Press, 1968; New York, Harper & Row, 1980.

———, REUVEN P. BULKA and WILLIAM S. SAHAKIAN, eds., *Logotherapy in Action*. Foreword by Viktor E. Frankl. New York, Jason Aronson, Inc., 1979.

FRANKL, VIKTOR E., *Man's Search for Meaning: An Introduction to Logotherapy*. Preface by Gordon W. Allport. Boston, Beacon Press, 1959; paperback edition, New York, Pocket Books, 1977.

———, *The Doctor and the Soul: From Psychotherapy to Logotherapy*. New York, Alfred A. Knopf, Inc.; second, expanded edition, 1965; paperback edition, New York, Vintage Books, 1977.

———, *Psychotherapy and Existentialism: Selected Papers on Logotherapy*. New York, Washington Square Press, 1967; Touchstone paperback, 1975.

————, *The Will to Meaning: Foundations and Applications of Logotherapy.* New York and Cleveland, The World Publishing Company, 1969; paperback edition, New York, New American Library, 1976.

————, *The Unconscious God: Psychotherapy and Theology.* New York, Simon and Schuster, 1978.

————, *The Unheard Cry for Meaning: Psychotherapy and Humanism.* New York, Simon and Schuster, 1978; Touchstone paperback, 1979.

————, *Synchronization in Buchenwald,* a play, offset, $5.00. Available at the Institute of Logotherapy, 1 Lawson Road, Berkeley, CA 94707.

LESLIE, ROBERT C., *Jesus and Logotherapy: The Ministry of Jesus as Interpreted Through the Psychotherapy of Viktor Frankl.* New York and Nashville, Abingdon Press, 1965; paperback edition, 1968.

TAKASHIMA, HIROSHI, *Psychosomatic Medicine and Logotherapy.* Foreword by Viktor E. Frankl. Oceanside, New York, Dabor Science Publications, 1977.

TWEEDIE, DONALD F., *Logotherapy and the Christian Faith: An Evaluation of Frankl's Existential Approach to Psychotherapy.* Preface by Viktor E. Frankl. Grand Rapids, Baker Book House, 1961; paperback edition, 1972.

————, *The Christian and the Couch: An Introduction to Christian Logotherapy.* Grand Rapids, Baker Book House, 1963.

UNGERSMA, AARON J., *The Search for Meaning: A New Approach in Psychotherapy and Pastoral Psychology.* Philadelphia, Westminster Press, 1961; paperback edition, Foreword by Viktor E. Frankl, 1968.

NOTE: In the following are listed selected books by Viktor E. Frankl published in German and not translated into English:

FRANKL, VIKTOR E., *Die Psychotherapie in der Praxis: Eine kasuistische Einführung für Ärzte.* Vienna, Deuticke, 1975.

————, *Anthropologische Grundlagen der Psychotherapie.* Bern, Huber, 1975.

————, *Theorie und Therapie der Neurosen: Einführung in Logotherapie und Existenzanalyse.* Munich, Reinhardt, 1975.

————, *Der Wille zum Sinn: Ausgewählte Vorträge über Logotherapie.* Bern, Huber, 1978.

————, *Psychotherapie für den Laien: Rundfunkvorträge über Seelenheilkunde.* Freiburg im Breisgau, Herder, 1978.

————, *Das Leiden am sinnlosen Leben: Psychotherapie für heute.* Freiburg im Breisgau, Herder, 1978.

————, *Der Mensch vor der Frage nach dem Sinn: Eine Auswahl aus dem Gesamtwerk.* Vorwort von Konrad Lorenz, Munich, Piper, 1979.

2. CHAPTERS IN BOOKS

ARNOLD, MAGDA B., and JOHN A. GASSON, "Logotherapy and Existential Analysis," in *The Human Person.* New York, Ronald Press, 1954.

ASCHER, L. MICHAEL, "Paradoxical Intention," in *Handbook of Behavior Intervention,* A. Goldstein and E. B. Foa, eds. New York, John Wiley, in press.

BARNITZ, HARRY W., "Frankl's Logotherapy," in *Existentialism and The New Christianity.* New York, Philosophical Library, 1969.

BRUNO, FRANK J., "The Will to Meaning," in *Human Adjustment and Personal Growth: Seven Pathways.* New York, John Wiley & Sons, Inc., 1977.

DOWNING, LESTER N., "Logotherapy," in *Counseling Theories and Techniques.* Chicago, Nelson-Hall, 1975.

ELLIS, ALBERT, and ELIOT ABRAHMS, "The Use of Humor and Paradoxical Intention," in *Brief Psychotherapy in Medical and Health Practice.* New York, Springer, 1978.

ELMORE, THOMAS M., and EUGENE D. CHAMBRES, "Anomie, Existential Neurosis and Personality: Relevance for Counseling," in *Proceedings,* 75th Annual Convention, American Psychological Association, 1967, 341–42.

FRANKL, VIKTOR E., Contributions to *Critical Incidents in Psychotherapy,* S. W. Standal and R. J. Corsini, eds. Englewood Cliffs, Prentice-Hall, 1959.

————, "Logotherapy and the Collective Neuroses," in *Progress in Psychotherapy,* J. H. Masserman and J. L. Moreno, eds. New York, Grune & Stratton, 1959.

————, "The Philosophical Foundations of Logotherapy" (paper

read before the first Lexington Conference on Phenomenology on April 4, 1963), in *Phenomenology: Pure and Applied,* Erwin Straus, ed. Pittsburgh, Duquesne University Press, 1964.

―――, "Fragments from the Logotherapeutic Treatment of Four Cases, With an Introduction and Epilogue by G. Kaczanowski," in *Modern Psychotherapeutic Practice: Innovations in Technique,* Arthur Burton, ed. Palo Alto, Science and Behavior Books, 1965.

―――, "The Will to Meaning," in *Are You Nobody?* Richmond, Virginia, John Knox Press, 1966.

―――, "Accepting Responsibility" and "Overcoming Circumstances," in *Man's Search for a Meaningful Faith: Selected Readings,* Judith Weidmann, ed. Nashville, Graded Press, 1967.

―――, "Comment on Vatican II's Pastoral Constitution on the Church in the Modern World, in *World.* Chicago, Catholic Action Federations, 1967.

―――, "Paradoxical Intention: A Logotherapeutic Technique," in *Active Psychotherapy,* Harold Greenwald, ed. New York, Atherton Press, 1967.

―――, "The Significance of Meaning for Health," in *Religion and Medicine: Essays on Meaning, Values and Health,* David Belgum, ed. Ames, Iowa, The Iowa State University Press, 1967.

―――, "The Task of Education in an Age of Meaninglessness," in *New Prospects for the Small Liberal Arts College,* Sidney S. Letter, ed. New York, Teachers College Press, 1968.

―――, "Self-Transcendence as a Human Phenomenon," in *Readings in Humanistic Psychology,* Anthony J. Sutich and Miles A. Vich, eds. New York, The Free Press, 1969.

―――, "Beyond Self-Actualization and Self-Expression," in *Perspectives on the Group Process: A Foundation for Counseling with Groups,* C. Gratton Kemp, ed. Boston, Houghton Mifflin Company, 1970.

―――, "Logotherapy," in *Psychopathology Today: Experimentation, Theory and Research.* William S. Sahakian, ed. Itasca, Illinois, F. E. Peacock Publishers, 1970.

―――, "Reductionism and Nihilism," in *Beyond Reductionism: New Perspectives in the Life Sciences* (The Alpbach Symposium, 1968), Arthur Koestler and J. R. Smythies, eds. New York, Macmillan, 1970.

―――, "Universities and the Quest for Peace," in *Report of the*

First World Conference on the Role of the University in the Quest for Peace. Binghamton, New York, State University of New York, 1970.

———, "What Is Meant by Meaning?" in *Values in an Age of Confrontation*, Jeremiah W. Canning, ed. Columbus, Ohio, Charles E. Merrill Publishing Company, 1970.

———, "Dynamics, Existence and Values" and "The Concept of Man in Logotherapy," in *Personality Theory: A Source Book*, Harold J. Vetter and Barry D. Smith, eds. New York, Appleton-Century-Crofts, 1971.

———, "Youth in Search of Meaning," in *Students Search for Meaning*, James Edward Doty, ed. Kansas City, Missouri, The Lowell Press, 1971.

———, "Address Before the Third Annual Meeting of the Academy of Religion and Mental Health," in *Discovering Man in Psychology: A Humanistic Approach*, Frank T. Severin, ed. New York, McGraw-Hill, Inc., 1973.

———, "Beyond Pluralism and Determinism," in *Unity Through Diversity: A Festschrift for Ludwig von Bertalanffy*, William Ray and Nicholas D. Rizzo, eds. New York, Gordon and Breach, 1973.

———, "Meaninglessness: A Challenge to Psychologists," in *Theories of Psychopathology and Personality*, Theodore Millon, ed. Philadelphia, W. B. Saunders Company, 1973.

———, "Encounter: The Concept and Its Vulgarization," in *Psychotherapy and Behavior Change 1973*, Hans H. Strupp *et al.*, eds. Chicago, Aldine Publishing Company, 1974.

———, "Paradoxical Intention and Dereflection: Two Logotherapeutic Techniques," in *New Dimensions in Psychiatry: A World View*, Silvano Arieti, ed. New York, John Wiley & Sons, Inc., 1975.

———, "Logotherapy," in *Encyclopaedic Handbook of Medical Psychology*, Stephen Krauss, ed. London and Boston, Butterworth, 1976.

———, "Man's Search of Ultimate Meaning," in *On the Way to Self-Knowledge*, Jacob Needleman, ed. New York, Alfred A. Knopf, Inc., 1976.

———, "The Depersonalization of Sex," in *Humanistic Psychology: A Source Book*, I. David Welch, George A. Tate and Fred

Richards, eds. Buffalo, New York, Prometheus Books, 1978.
———, "Logotherapy," in *The Psychotherapy Handbook,* Richie Herink, ed. New York, New American Library, 1980.

FREILICHER, M., "Applied Existential Psychology: Viktor Frankl and Logotherapy," in *PsychoSources,* Evelyn Shapiro, ed. New York, Bantam Books, 1973.

FREY, DAVID H., and FREDERICK E. HESLET, "Viktor Frankl," in *Existential Theory for Counselors.* Boston, Houghton Mifflin Company, 1975.

FRIEDMAN, MAURICE, "Viktor Frankl," in *The Worlds of Existentialism.* New York, Random House, 1964.

GALE, RAYMOND F., "Logotherapy," in *Who Are You? The Psychology of Being Yourself.* Englewood Cliffs, Prentice-Hall, 1974.

HOWLAND, ELIHU S., "Viktor Frankl," in *Speak Through the Earthquake: Religious Faith and Emotional Health.* Philadelphia, United Church Press, 1972.

KIERNAN, THOMAS, "Logotherapy," in *Shrinks, etc.: A Consumer's Guide to Psychotherapies.* New York, The Dial Press, 1974.

KORCHIN, SIDNEY J., "Logotherapy," in *Modern Clinical Psychology.* New York, Basic Books, Inc., 1976.

LANDE, NATHANIEL, "Logotherapy (Viktor Frankl)," in *Mindstyles, Lifestyles: A Comprehensive Overview of Today's Life-Changing Philosophies.* Los Angeles, Price, Stern, Sloan, 1976.

LEDERMANN, E. K., "Viktor E. Frankl's Ontological Value Ethics," in *Existential Neurosis.* London, Butterworth, 1972.

LESLIE, ROBERT, "Frankl's New Concept of Man," in *Contemporary Religious Issues,* Donald E. Hartsock, ed. Belmont, California, Wadsworth Publishing Company, 1968.

LISTON, ROBERT A., "Viktor Frankl," in *Healing the Mind: Eight Views of Human Nature.* New York, Praeger, 1974.

McCARTHY COLMAN, "Viktor Frankl," in *Inner Companions.* Washington, D.C., Acropolis Books Ltd., 1975.

McKINNEY, FRED, "Man's Search for Meaning," in *Psychology in Action.* New York, Macmillan, 1967.

MARKS, ISAAC M., "Paradoxical Intention ('Logotherapy'), in *Fears and Phobias.* New York, Academic Press, 1969.

———, "Paradoxical Intention," in *Behavior Modification,* W. Stewart Agras, ed. Boston, Little, Brown and Company, 1972.

————, "Paradoxical Intention (Logotherapy)," in *Encyclopaedic Handbook of Medical Psychology,* Stephen Krauss, ed. London and Boston, Butterworth, 1976.

MASLOW, ABRAHAM H., "Comments on Dr. Frankl's Paper," in *Readings in Humanistic Psychology,* Anthony J. Sutich and Miles A. Vich, eds. New York, The Free Press, 1969.

MATSON, KATINKA, "Viktor E. Frankl Logotherapy," in *The Psychology Omnibook of Personal Development.* New York, William Morrow and Company, Inc., 1977.

MISIAK, HENRY, and VIRGINIA STAUDT SEXTON, "Logotherapy," in *Phenomenological, Existential, and Humanistic Psychologies: A Historical Survey.* New York, Grune & Stratton, 1973.

PAGE, JAMES D., "Frankl," in *Psychopathology.* Chicago, Adline Publishing Company, second edition, 1975.

PATTERSON, C. H., "Frankl's Logotherapy," in *Theories of Counseling and Psychotherapy.* New York, Harper & Row, 1966.

PRICE, JOHANNA, "Existential Theories: Viktor Frankl," in *Abnormal Psychology: Current Perspectives.* Del Mar, California, Communication Research Machines, 1972.

REYNOLDS, DAVID K., "Logotherapy," in *Morita Psychotherapy.* Berkeley, University of California Press, 1976.

SAHAKIAN, WILLIAM S., "Viktor Frankl," in *History of Psychology.* Itasca, Illinois, F. E. Peacock Publishers, Inc., 1969.

————, "Logotherapy," in *Psychotherapy and Counseling: Studies in Technique.* Chicago, Rand McNally, 1969.

————, "Logotherapy Approach to Personality," in *Psychology of Personality.* Chicago, Rand McNally, 1974.

————, "Logotherapy: The Will to Meaning," in *History and Systems of Psychology.* New York, John Wiley & Sons, Inc., 1975.

————, and MABEL LEWIS SAHAKIAN, "Viktor E. Frankl: Will to Meaning," in *Realms of Philosophy.* Cambridge, Massachusetts, Schenkman Publishing Company, Inc., 1974.

SALIT, NORMAN, "Existential Analysis: Logotherapy—the Gulf Narrows," in *The Worlds of Norman Salit,* Abraham Burstein, ed. New York, Bloch, 1966.

SCHILLING, S. PAUL, " 'The Unconscious God': Viktor Frankl," in *God Incognito.* Nashville and New York, Abingdon Press, 1974.

SCHNEIDER, MARIUS G., "The Existentialistic Concept of the

Human Person in Viktor E. Frankl's Logotherapy." in *Heirs and Ancestors,* John K. Ryan, ed. Washington, D.C., Catholic University of America Press, 1973.

SPIEGELBERG, HERBERT, "Viktor Frankl: Phenomenology in Logotherapy and *Existenzanalyse,*" in *Phenomenology in Psychology and Psychiatry.* Evanston, Illinois, Northwestern University Press, 1972.

STRUNK, ORLO, "Religious Maturity and Viktor Frankl," in *Mature Religion.* New York, and Nashville, Abingdon Press, 1965.

TYRELL, BERNARD J., "Logotherapy and Christotherapy," in *Christotherapy: Healing through Enlightenment.* New York, The Seabury Press, 1975.

VANDERVELDT, JAMES H., and ROBERT P. ODENWALD, "Existential Analysis," in *Psychiatry and Catholicism.* New York, McGraw-Hill, 1952.

VARMA, VED, "Egotherapy, Logotherapy and Religious Therapy," in *Psychology Today.* London, Constable, 1974.

ZAVALLONI, ROBERTO, "Human Freedom and Logotherapy," in *Self-Determination.* Chicago, Forum Books, 1962.

3. ARTICLES AND MISCELLANEOUS

ANSBACHER, ROWENA R., "The Third Viennese School of Psychotherapy." *Journal of Individual Psychology,* XV (1959), 236–37.

ASCHER, L. MICHAEL, "Employing Paradoxical Intention in the Behavioral Treatment of Urinary Retention." *Scandinavian Journal of Behavior Therapy,* Vol. 6, Suppl. 4 (1977), 28.

———, "Paradoxical Intention: A Review of Preliminary Research." *The International Forum for Logotherapy,* Volume 1, Number 1 (Winter 1978–Spring 1979), 18–21.

———, "Paradoxical Intention in the Treatment of Urinary Retention." *Behavior Research & Therapy,* Vol. 17 (1979), 267–70.

———, "Paradoxical Intention Viewed by a Behavior Therapist." *The International Forum for Logotherapy,* Volume 1, Number 3 (Spring 1980), 13–16.

————, "Paradoxical Intention and Insomnia: An Experimental Investigation." *Behavior Research & Therapy,* Vol. 17 (1979), 408–11.

————, and JAY S. EFRAN, "Use of Paradoxical Intention in a Behavior Program for Sleep Onset Insomnia." *Journal of Consulting and Clinical Psychology,* (1978), 747–50.

————, and RALPH MacMILLAN TURNER, "A Comparison of Two Methods for the Administration of Paradoxical Intention." *Behavior Research & Therapy,* Vol. 18 (1980), 121–26.

BALLARD, R. E., "An Empirical Investigation of Viktor Frankl's Concept of the Search for Meaning: A Pilot Study with a Sample of Tuberculosis Patients." Doctoral dissertation, Michigan State University, 1965.

BAZZI, TULLIO, "A Center of Logotherapy in Italy." *The International Forum for Logotherapy,* Volume 1, Number 3 (Spring 1980), 26–27.

————, "Paradoxical Intention and Autogenic Training—Convergence or Incompatibility?" *The International Forum for Logotherapy,* Volume 2, Number 2 (Summer-Fall 1979), 35–37.

BIRNBAUM, FERDINAND, "Frankl's Existential Psychology from the Viewpoint of Individual Psychology." *Journal of Individual Psychology,* XVII (1961), 162–66.

BÖCKMAN, WALTER, "Logotherapy as a Theory of Culture." *The International Forum for Logotherapy,* Volume 1, Number 3 (Spring 1980), 44–45.

BORDELEAU, LOUIS-GABRIEL, *"La Relation entre les valeurs de choix vocationnel et les valeurs creatrices chez V. E. Frankl."* Doctoral dissertation, University of Ottawa, 1971.

BULKA, REUVEN P., "An Analysis of the Viability of Frankl's Logotherapeutic System as a Secular Theory." Thesis presented to the Department of Religious Studies of the University of Ottawa as partial fulfillment of the requirements for the degree of Master of Arts, 1969.

————, "Denominational Implications of the Religious Nature of Logotherapy." Thesis presented to the Department of Religious Studies of the University of Ottawa as partial fulfillment of the requirements for the degree of Doctor of Philosophy, 1971.

————, "Logotherapy and Judaism." *Jewish Spectator,* XXXVII, No. 7 (Sept. 1972), 17–19.

———, "Logotherapy and Judaism—Some Philosophical Comparisons." *Tradition,* XII (1972), 72–89.

———, "Death in Life—Talmudic and Logotherapeutic Affirmations." *Humanitas (Journal of the Institute of Man),* X, No. 1 (Feb. 1974), 33–42.

———, "The Ecumenical Ingredient in Logotherapy." *Journal of Ecumenical Studies,* XI, No. 1 (Winter 1974), 13–24.

———, "Logotherapy as a Response to the Holocaust." *Tradition,* XV (1975), 89–96.

———, "Logotherapy and Talmudic Judaism." *Journal of Religion and Health,* XIV (1975), No. 4, 277–83.

———, "Logotherapy and the Talmud on Suffering: Clinical and Meta-Clinical Perspectives." *Journal of Psychology and Judaism,* Vol. 2, No. 1 (Fall 1977), 31–44.

———, "Logotherapy—A Step Beyond Freud: Its Relevance for Jewish Thought." *Jewish Life,* Fall, Winter 1977–78, 46–53.

———, "Is Logotherapy A Spiritual Therapy?" *Association of Mental Health Clergy Forum,* Vol. 30, No. 2 (Jan. 1978).

———, "The Work Situation: Logotherapeutic and Talmudic Perspectives." *Journal of Psychology and Judaism,* Vol. 2, No. 2 (Spring 1978), 52–61.

———, "Hasidism and Logotherapy: Encounter Through Anthology." *Journal of Psychology and Judaism,* Vol 3, No. 1 (Fall 1978), 60–74.

———, "Is Logotherapy Authoritarian?" *Journal of Humanistic Psychology,* Vol. 18, No. 4 (Fall 1978), 45–54.

———, "Frankl's Impact on Jewish Life and Thought." *The International Forum for Logotherapy,* Vol. 1, No. 3 (Spring 1980), 41–43.

———, "The Upside-down Thumb: Talmudic Thinking and Logotherapy." *Voices: Journal of the American Academy of Psychotherapy,* Vol. 16 (Spring 1980), 70–74.

BURCK, JAMES LESTER, "The Relevance of Viktor Frankl's 'Will to Meaning' for Preaching to Juvenile Delinquents." A Master of Theology thesis submitted to the Southern Baptist Theological Seminary, Louisville. Kentucky, 1966.

CALABRESE, EDWARD JAMES, "The Evolutionary Basis of Logotherapy." Dissertation, University of Massachusetts, 1974.

CARRIGAN, THOMAS EDWARD, "The Meaning of Meaning in Logotherapy of Dr. Viktor E. Frankl." Thesis presented to the

School of Graduate Studies as partial fulfillment of the requirements for the degree of Master of Arts in Philosophy, University of Ottawa, Canada, 1973.

CAVANAGH, MICHAEL E., "The Relationship between Frankl's 'Will to Meaning' and the Discrepancy Between the Actual Self and the Ideal Self." Doctoral dissertation, University of Ottawa, 1966.

CHASTAIN, MILLS KENT, "The Unfinished Revolution: Logotherapy as Applied to Primary Grades 1–4 Values Clarification in the Social Studies Curriculum in Thailand." Thesis, Monterey Institute of International Studies, 1979.

COHEN, DAVID, "The Frankl Meaning." *Human Behavior*, Vol. 6, No. 7 (Jul. 1977), 56–62.

COLLEY, CHARLES SANFORD, "An Examination of Five Major Movements in Counseling Theory in Terms of How Representative Theorists (Freud, Williamson, Wolpe, Rogers and Frankl) View the Nature of Man." Dissertation, University of Alabama, 1970.

CRUMBAUGH, JAMES C., "The Application of Logotherapy." *Journal of Existentialism*, V (1965), 403–12.

———, "Cross Validation of Purpose-in-Life Test Based on Frankl's Concepts." *Journal of Individual Psychology*, XXIV (1968), 74–81.

———, "Frankl's Logotherapy: A New Orientation in Counseling." *Journal of Religion and Health*, X (1971), 373–86.

———, "Aging and Adjustment: The Applicability of Logotherapy and the Purpose-in-Life Test." *The Geronotologist*, XII (1972), 418-20.

———, "Changes in Frankl's existential vacuum as a measure of therapeutic outcome." *Newsletter for Research in Psychology* (Veterans Administration Center, Bay Pines, Florida), Vol. 14, No. 2 (May 1972), 35–37.

———, "Frankl's Logotherapy: An Answer to the Crisis in Identity." *Newsletter of the Mississippi Personnel & Guidance Association*, IV, No. 2 (Oct. 1972), 3.

———, "Patty's Purpose: Perversion of Frankl's Search for Meaning." *J. Graphoanalysis*, July 1976, 12–13.

———, "Logoanalysis." *Uniquest* (The First Unitarian Church of Berkeley), No. 7 (1977), 38–39.

———, "The Seeking of Noetic Goals Test (SONG): A Complementary Scale to the Purpose in Life Test (PIL)." *Journal of Clinical Psychology,* Vol. 33, No. 3 (Jul. 1977), 900–07.

———, "Logotherapy as a Bridge Between Religion and Psychotherapy." *Journal of Religion and Health,* Vol. 18, No. 3 (Jul. 1979), 188–191.

———, and LEONARD T. MAHOLICK, "The Case for Frankl's 'Will to Meaning.' " *Journal of Existential Psychiatry,* IV (1963), 43–48.

———, "An Experimental Study in Existentialism: The Psychometric Approach to Frankl's Concept of Noögenic Neurosis." *Journal of Clinical Psychology,* XX (1964), 200–07.

———, SISTER MARY RAPHAEL and RAYMOND R. SHRADER, "Frankl's Will to Meaning in a Religious Order" (delivered before Division 24, American Psychological Association, at the annual convention in San Francisco, August 30, 1968). *Journal of Clinical Psychology,* XXVI (1970), 206–07.

———, and GORDON L. CARR, "Treatment of Alcoholics with Logotherapy." *The International Journal of the Addictions,* Vol. 14, No. 6 (1979), 847–53.

DANSART, BERNARD. "Development of a Scale to Measure Attitudinal Values as Defined by Viktor Frankl." Dissertation, Northern Illinois University, De Kalb, 1974.

DICKSON, CHARLES W., "Logotherapy and the Redemptive Encounter." *Dialogue,* Spring 1974, 110–14.

———, "Logotherapy as a Pastoral Tool." *Journal of Religion and Health,* XIV, No. 3, (1975), 207–13.

"The Doctor and the Soul: Dr. Viktor Frankl." *Harvard Medical Alumni Bulletin,* XXXVI, No. 1 (Fall 1961), 8.

DUNCAN, FRANKLIN D., "Logotherapy and the Pastoral Care of Physically Disabled Persons." A thesis in the Department of Psychology of Religion submitted to the faculty of the Graduate School of Theology in partial fulfillment of the requirements for the degree of Master of Theology at Southern Baptist Theological Seminary, Louisville, Kentucky, 1968.

EGER, EDITH EVA, "Viktor Frankl & Me." *Association for Humanistic Psychology Newsletter,* February 1976, 15–16.

EISENBERG, MIGNON, "The Logotherapeutic Intergenerational Communications Group." *The International Forum for Logotherapy,* Vol. 1, No. 2 (Summer-Fall 1979), 23–25.

———, "Logotherapy and the College Student." *The International Forum for Logotherapy,* Vol. 1, No. 3 (Spring 1980), 22–24.

———, "My 'Second Meeting' with Viktor Frankl." *The International Forum for Logotherapy,* Vol. 1, No. 3 (Spring 1980), 53–54.

———, "The Logotherapeutic Intergenerational Encounter Group: A Phenomenological Approach." Dissertation, Southeastern University, New Orleans, 1980.

ENG, ERLING, "The Akedah, Oedipus, and Dr. Frankl." *Psychotherapy: Theory, Research and Practice,* Vol. 16, No. 3 (Fall, 1979), 269–71.

FABRY, JOSEPH, "A Most Ingenious Paradox." *The Register-Leader of the Unitarian Universalist Association,* Vol. 149 (Jun. 1967), 7–8.

———, "The Defiant Power of the Human Spirit." *The Christian Ministry,* Mar. 1972, 35–36.

———, "Application of Logotherapy in Small Sharing Groups." *Journal of Religion and Health,* XIII (1974), No. 2, 128–36.

———, "Logotherapy and Eastern Religions." *Journal of Religion and Health,* XIV (1975), No. 4, 271–76.

———, "Aspects and Prospects of Logotherapy: A Dialogue with Viktor Frankl." *The International Forum for Logotherapy,* Vol. 1, No. 1 (Winter 1978–Spring 1979), 3–6.

———, "Three Faces of Frankl." *The International Forum for Logotherapy,* Vol. 1, No. 3 (Spring 1980), 40.

———, and MAX KNIGHT (pseud. PETER FABRIZIUS), "Viktor Frankl's Logotherapy." *Delphian Quarterly,* XLVII, No. 3 (1964), 27–30.

———, "The Use of Humor in Therapy." *Delphian Quarterly,* XLVIII, No. 3 (1965), 22–36.

FARR, ALAN P., "Logotherapy and Senior Adults." *The International Forum for Logotherapy,* Vol. 1, No. 1 (Winter 1978–Spring 1979), 14–17.

"The Father of Logotherapy." *Existential Psychiatry,* Vol. 1 (1967), 439.

FORSTMEYER, ANNEMARIE VON, "The Will to Meaning as a Prerequisite for Self-Actualization." Thesis presented to the faculty of California Western University, San Diego, in partial fulfillment of the requirements for the degree Master of Arts, 1968.

FOX, DOUGLAS A., "Logotherapy and Religion." *Religion in Life,* XXXI (1965), 235–44.

FRANKL, VIKTOR E., "Logos and Existence in Psychotherapy." *American Journal of Psychotherapy,* VII (1953), 8–15.

———, "Group Psychotherapeutic Experiences in a Concentration Camp" (paper read before the Second International Congress of Psychotherapy, Leiden, Netherlands, Sep. 8, 1951). *Group Psychotherapy,* VII (1954), 81–90.

———, "The Concept of Man in Psychotherapy" (paper read before the Royal Society of Medicine, Section of Psychiatry, London, England, June 15, 1944). *Pastoral Psychology,* VI (1955), 16–26.

———, "From Psychotherapy to Logotherapy." *Pastoral Psychology,* VII (1956), 56–60.

———, "Guest Editorial." *Academy Reporter,* III, No. 5 (May 1958), 1–4.

———, "On Logotherapy and Existential Analysis" (paper read before the Association for the Advancement of Psychoanalysis, New York, April 17, 1957), *American Journal of Psychoanalysis,* XVIII (1958), 28–37.

———, "The Search for Meaning." *Saturday Review* (Sep. 13, 1958).

———, "The Will to Meaning." *Journal of Pastoral Care,* XII (1958), 82–88.

———, "The Spiritual Dimension in Existential Analysis and Logotherapy" (paper read before the Fourth International Congress of Psychotherapy, Barcelona, Sep. 5, 1958). *Journal of Individual Psychology,* XV (1959), 157–65.

———, "Beyond Self-Actualization and Self-Expression" (paper read before the Conference on Existential Psychotherapy, Chicago, Dec. 13, 1959). *Journal of Existential Psychiatry,* I (1960), 5–20.

———, "Paradoxical Intention: A Logotherapeutic Technique" (paper read before the American Association for the Advancement of Psychotherapy, New York, Feb. 26, 1960). *American Journal of Psychotherapy,* XIV (1960), 520–35.

———, "Dynamics, Existence and Values." *Journal of Existential Psychiatry,* II (1961), 5–16.

———, "Logotherapy and the Challenge of Suffering" (paper read before the American Conference on Existential Psychotherapy,

New York, Feb. 27, 1960). *Review of Existential Psychology and Psychiatry,* I (1961), 3–7.

———, "Psychotherapy and Philosophy." *Philosophy Today,* V (1961), 59–64.

———, "Religion and Existential Psychotherapy." *Gordon Review,* VI (1961), 2–10.

———, "Basic Concepts of Logotherapy," *Journal of Existential Psychiatry,* III (1962), 111–18.

———, "Logotherapy and the Challenge of Suffering." *Pastoral Psychology,* XIII (1962), 25–28.

———, "Psychiatry and Man's Quest for Meaning." *Journal of Religion and Health,* I (1962), 93–103.

———, "The Will to Meaning." *Living Chruch,* CXLIV (June 24, 1962), 8–14.

———, "Angel as Much as Beast: Man Transcends Himself." *Unitarian Universalist Register-Leader,* CXLIV (Feb. 1963), 8–9.

———, "Existential Dynamics and Neurotic Escapism" (paper read before the Conference on Existential Psychiatry, Toronto, May 6, 1962). *Journal of Existential Psychiatry,* IV (1963), 27–42.

———, "Existential Escapism." *Motive,* XXIV (Jan.-Feb. 1964), 11–14.

———, "In Steady Search for Meaning." *Liberal Dimension,* II, No. 2 (1964), 3–8.

———, "The Will to Meaning" (paper read before the Conference on Phenomenology, Lexington, April 4, 1963). *Christian Century,* LXXI (April 22, 1964), 515–17.

———, "How a Sense of a Task in Life Can Help You Over the Bumps." *The National Observer,* July 12, 1964, 22.

———, "The Concept of Man in Logotherapy" (175th Anniversary Lecture, Georgetown University, Washington, D.C., February 27, 1964.) *Journal of Existentialism,* VI (1965), 53–58.

———, "Logotherapy—A New Psychology of Man." *The Gadfly,* Vol. 17, Issue 1 (Dec. 1965–Jan. 1966).

———, "Logotherapy and Existential Analysis: A Review" (paper read before the Symposium on Logotherapy, 6th International Congress of Psychotherapy, London, August 26, 1964). *American Journal of Psychotherapy,* XX (1966), 252–60.

———, "Self-Transcendence As a Human Phenomenon." *Journal of Humanistic Psychology,* VI, No. 2 (Fall 1966), 97–106.

————, "Time and Responsibility." *Existential Psychiatry*, I (1966), 361–66.

————, "What Is Meant by Meaning?" *Journal of Existentialism*, VII, No. 25 (Fall 1966), 21–28.

————, "Logotherapy." *The Israel Annals of Psychiatry and Related Disciplines*, VII (1967), 142–55.

————, "Logotherapy and Existentialism." *Psychotherapy: Theory, Research and Practice*, IV, No. 3 (Aug. 1967), 138–42.

————, "What Is a Man?" *Life Association News*, LXII, No. 9 (Sep. 1967), 151–57.

————, "Experiences in a Concentration Camp." *Jewish Heritage*, XI (1968), 5–7.

————, "The Search for Meaning" (abstract from a series of lectures given at the Brandeis Institute in California). *Jewish Heritage*, XI (1968), 8–11.

————, "The Cosmos and the Mind. (How Far Can We Go?) A Dialogue with Geoffrey Frost." *Pace*, V, No. 8 (Aug. 1969), 34–39.

————, "Eternity Is the Here and Now." *Pace*, V, No. 4 (April 1969), 2.

————, "Youth in Search for Meaning" (Third Paul Dana Bartlett Memorial Lecture). *The Baker World (The Baker University Newsletter)*, I, No. 4 (Jan. 1969), 2–5.

————, "Entering the Human Dimension." *Attitude*, I (1970), 2–6.

————, "Fore-Runner of Existential Psychiatry." *Journal of Individual Psychology*, XXVI (1970), 12.

————, "Determinism and Humanism." *Humanitas (Journal of the Institute of Man)*, VII (1971), 23–26.

————, "Existential Escapism." *Omega*, Vol. 2, No. 4 (Nov. 1971), 307–311.

————, "The Feeling of Meaninglessness: A Challenge to Psychotherapy." *The American Journal of Psychoanalysis*, XXXII, No. 1 (1972), 85–89.

————, "Man in Search of Meaning." *Widening Horizons* (Rockford College), Vol. 8, No. 5 (Aug. 1972).

————, "Encounter: The Concept and Its Vulgarization." *The Journal of the American Academy of Psychoanalysis*, I, No. 1 (1973), 73–83.

————, "The Depersonalization of Sex." *Synthesis (The Realization of the Self)*, I (Spring 1974), 7–11.

————, "Paradoxical Intention and Dereflection." *Psychotherapy: Theory, Research and Practice,* XII, No. 3 (Fall 1975), 226–37.

————, "A Psychiatrist Looks at Love." *Uniquest* (The First Unitarian Church of Berkeley), No. 5 (1976), 6–9.

————, "Some Thoughts on the Painful Wisdom." *Uniquest* (The First Unitarian Church of Berkeley), No. 6 (1976), 3.

————, "Survival—for What?" *Uniquest* (The First Unitarian Church of Berkeley), No. 6 (1976), 38.

————, "Logotherapy." *The International Forum for Logotherapy,* Vol. 1, No. 1 (Winter 1978–Spring 1979), 22–23.

————, "Endogenous Depression and Noögenic Neurosis (Case Histories and Comments)." *The International Forum for Logotherapy,* Vol. 2, No. 2 (Summer-Fall 1979), 38–40.

GARFIELD, CHARLES A., "A Psychometric and Clinical Investigation of Frankl's Concept of Existential Vacuum and of Anomie." *Psychiatry,* XXXVI (1973), 396–408.

GERZ, HANS O., "The Treatment of the Phobic and the Obsessive-Compulsive Patient Using Paradoxical Intention sec. Viktor E. Frankl." *Journal of Neuropsychiatry,* III, No. 6 (July-Aug. 1962), 375–87.

————, "Experience with the Logotherapeutic Technique of Paradoxical Intention in the Treatment of Phobic and Obsessive-Compulsive Patients" (paper read at the Symposium of Logotherapy at the 6th International Congress of Psychotherapy, London, England, August 1964). *American Journal of Psychiatry,* CXXIII, No. 5 (Nov. 1966), 548–53.

————, "Reply," *American Journal of Psychiatry,* CXXIII, No. 10 (Apr. 1967), 1306.

GILL, AJAIPAL SINGH, "An Appraisal of Viktor E. Frankl's Theory of Logotherapy as a Philosophical Base for Education." Dissertation, The American University, 1970.

GLEASON, JOHN J., "Lucy and Logotherapy: A Context, a Concept, and a Case." *Voices: The Art and Science of Psychotherapy,* Vol. 7 (1971), 57–62.

GREEN, HERMAN H., "The 'Existential Vacuum' and the Pastoral Care of Elderly Widows in a Nursing Home." Master's thesis, Southern Baptist Theological Seminary, Louisville, Kentucky, 1970.

GROLLMAN, EARL A., "Viktor E. Frankl: A Bridge Between

Psychiatry and Religion." *Conservative Judaism*, XIX, No. 1 (Fall 1964), 19–23.

———, "The Logotherapy of Viktor E. Frankl." *Judaism*, XIV (1965), 22–38.

GROSSMAN, NATHAN, "The Rabbi and the Doctor of the Soul." *Jewish Spectator*, XXXIV, No. 1 (Jan. 1969), 8–12.

GULDBRANDSEN, FRANCIS ALOYSIUS, "Some of the Pedagogical Implications in the Theoretical Work of Viktor Frankl in Existential Psychology: A Study in the Philosophic Foundations of Education." Doctoral dissertation, Michigan State University, 1972.

HALL, MARY HARRINGTON, "A Conversation with Viktor Frankl of Vienna." *Psychology Today*, I, No. 9 (Feb. 1968), 56–63.

HARRINGTON, DONALD SZANTHO, "The View from the Existential Vacuum," *Academy Reporter*, IX, No. 9 (Dec. 1964), 1–4.

HAVENS, LESTON L., "Paradoxical Intention." *Psychiatry & Social Science Review*, II (1968), 16–19.

HAWORTH, D. SWAN, "Viktor Frankl." *Judaism*, XIV (1965), 351–52.

HENDERSON, J. T., "The Will to Meaning of Viktor Frankl as a Meaningful Factor of Personality." Master's thesis, The University of Maryland, 1970.

HOLMES, R. M., "Meaning and Responsibility: A Comparative Analysis of the Concept of the Responsible Self in Search of Meaning in the Thought of Viktor Frankl and H. Richard Niebuhr with Certain Implications for the Church's Ministry to the University." Doctoral dissertation, Pacific School of Religion, Berkeley, California, 1965.

———, "Alcoholics Anonymous as Group Logotherapy." *Pastoral Psychology*, XXI (1970), 30–36.

HUMBERGER, FRANK E., "Practical Logotherapeutic Techniques." *Uniquest* (The First Unitarian Church of Berkeley), No. 7 (1977), 24–25.

———, "Logotherapy in Outplacement Counseling." *The International Forum for Logotherapy*, Vol. 1, No. 3 (Spring 1980), 50–53.

HYMAN, WILLIAM, "Practical Aspects of Logotherapy in Neurosurgery." *Existential Psychiatry*, VII (1969), 99–101.

JOHNSON, PAUL E., "Logotherapy: A Corrective for Determinism." *Christian Advocate*, V (Nov. 23, 1961), 12–13.

————, "Meet Doctor Frankl." *Adult Student*, XXIV (Oct. 1964), 8–10.

————, "The Meaning of Logotherapy." *Adult Student*, XXVI, No. 8 (Apr. 1967), 4–5.

————, "The Challenge of Logotherapy." *Journal of Religion and Health*, VII (1968), 122–30.

JONES, ELBERT WHALEY, "Nietzsche and Existential Analysis." Dissertation in the Department of Philosophy submitted to the faculty of the Graduate School of Arts and Sciences in partial fulfillment of the requirements for the degree of Master of Arts, New York University, 1967.

KACZANOWSKI, GODFRYD, "Frankl's Logotherapy." *American Journal of Psychiatry*, CXVII (1960), 563.

————, "Logotherapy—A New Psychotherapeutic Tool." *Psychosomatics*, Vol. 8 (May–Jun. 1967), 158–61.

KELZER, KENNETH, FRANCES VAUGHAN, and RICHARD GORRINGE, "Viktor Frankl: A Precursor for Transpersonal Psychotherapy." *The International Forum for Logotherapy*, Vol. 1, No. 3 (Spring 1980), 32–35.

KLAPPER, NAOMI, "On Being Human: A Comparative Study of Abraham J. Heschel and Viktor Frankl." Doctoral dissertation, Jewish Theological Seminary of America, New York, 1973.

KLITZKE, LOUIS L., "Students in Emerging Africa: Humanistic Psychology and Logotherapy in Tanzania," *Journal of Humanistic Psychology*, IX (1969), 105–26.

KOSUKEGAWA, TSUGIO, "A Comparative Study of the Differences Between Christian Existence and Secular Existence, and of Their Existential Frustration." *Japanese Journal of Educational and Social Psychology*, VII, No. 2 (1968), 195–208.

LAMONTAGNE, IVES, "Treatment of Erythrophobia by Paradoxical Intention." *The Journal of Nervous and Mental Disease*, Vol. 166, No. 4 (1978), 304–06.

LAPINSOHN, LEONARD, I., "Relationship of the Logotherapeutic Concepts of Anticipatory Anxiety and Paradoxical Intention to the Neurophysiological Theory of Induction." *Behavioral Neuropsychiatry*, III, No. 304 (1971), 12–14 and 24.

LESLIE, ROBERT C., "Viktor Frankl and C. G. Jung." *Shiggaion*, Vol. X, No. 2 (Dec. 1961).

————, "Viktor E. Frankl's New Concept of Man." *Motive,* XXII (1962), 16–19.

LEVINSON, JAY IRWIN, "An Investigation of Existential Vacuum in Grief via Widowhood." Dissertation, United States International University, San Diego, California, 1979.

————, "A Combination of Paradoxical Intention and Dereflection." *The International Forum for Logotherapy,* Vol. 2, No. 2 (Summer-Fall 1979), 40–41.

LUKAS, ELISABETH S., "The Four Steps of Logotherapy." *Uniquest* (The First Unitarian Church of Berkeley), No. 7 (1977), 24–25.

————, "The 'Ideal' Logotherapist—Three Contradictions." *The International Forum for Logotherapy,* Vol. 2, No. 2 (Summer-Fall 1979), 3–7.

MARRER, ROBERT F., "Existential-Phenomenological Foundations in Logotherapy Applicable to Counseling." Dissertation, Ohio University, 1972.

MASLOW, A. H., "Comments on Dr. Frankl's Paper." *Journal of Humanistic Psychology,* VI (1966), 107–12.

"Meaning in Life." *Time* (Feb. 2, 1968), 38–40.

MEIER, AUGUSTINE, "Frankl's 'Will to Meaning' as Measured by the Purpose-in-Life Test in Relation to Age and Sex Differences." Dissertation presented to The University of Ottawa, 1973.

————, "Frankl's 'Will to Meaning' as Measured by the Purpose-in-Life Test in Relation to Age and Sex Differences." *Journal of Clinical Psychology,* XXX (1974), 384–86.

MUILENBERG, DON T., "Meaning in Life: Its Significance in Psychotherapy." A dissertation presented to the faculty of the Graduate School, University of Missouri, 1968.

MÜLLER-HEGEMANN, D., "Methodological Approaches in Psychotherapy: Current Concepts in East Germany." *American Journal of Psychotherapy,* XVII (1963), 554–68.

MURPHY, LEONARD, "Extent of Purpose-in-Life and Four Frankl-Proposed Life Objectives." Doctoral dissertation in Department of Psychology, The University of Ottawa, 1967.

MURPHY, MARIBETH L., "Viktor Frankl: The New Phenomenology of Meaning." *The U.S.I.U. Doctoral Society Journal,* III, No. 2 (Jun. 1970), 1–10, and IV, No. 1 (Winter 1970–71), 45–46.

NEWTON, JOSEPH R., "Therapeutic Paradoxes, Paradoxical Intentions, and Negative Practice." *American Journal of Psychotherapy*, XXII (1968), 68–81.

NOONAN, J. ROBERT, "A Note on an Eastern Counterpart of Frankl's Paradoxical Intention." *Psychologia*, XII (1969), 147–49.

OFFUTT, BERCH R., HANDALL, "Logotherapy, Actualization Therapy or Contextual Self-Realization?" Dissertation, United States International University, 1975.

O'CONNELL, WALTER E., "Viktor Frankl, the Adlerian?" *Psychiatric Spectator*, Vol. VI, No. 11 (1970), 13–14.

———, "Frankl, Adler, and Spirituality." *Journal of Religion and Health*, XI (1972), 134–38.

"Originator of Logotherapy Discusses Its Basic Premises" (interview). *Roche Report: Frontiers of Clinical Psychiatry*, Vol. 5, No. 1 (Jan. 1, 1968), 5–6.

PALMA, ROBERT J., "Viktor E. Frankl: Multilevel Analyses and Complementarity." *Journal of Religion and Health*, XV (1976), 12–25.

PAREJA-HERRERA, GUILLERMO, "Logotherapy and Social Change." *The International Forum for Logotherapy*, Vol. 1, No. 3 (Spring 1980), 38–39.

PETRAROJA, SERGIO D., "The Concept of Freedom in Viktor Frankl." *Catholic Psychological Record*, Vol. 4 (Fall 1966).

PERVIN, LAWRENCE A., "Existentialism, Psychology, and Psychotherapy." *American Psychologist*, XV (1960), 305–09.

POLAK, PAUL, "Frankl's Existential Analysis." *American Journal of Psychotherapy*, III (1949), 517–22.

———, "The Anthropological Foundations of Logotherapy." *The International Forum for Logotherapy*, Vol. 1, No. 3 (Spring 1980), 46–48.

POPIELSKI, KAZIMIERZ, "Karol Wojtyla and Logotherapy." *The International Forum for Logotherapy*, Vol. 1, No. 3 (Spring 1980), 36–37.

QUIRK, JOHN M., "A Practical Outline of An Eight-Week Logogroup." *The International Forum for Logotherapy*, Vol. 2, No. 2 (Summer-Fall 1979), 15–22.

RASKIN, DAVID E., and ZANVEL E. KLEIN, "Losing a Symptom Through Keeping It: A Review of Paradoxical Treatment Techniques and Rationale." *Archives of General Psychiatry*, Vol. 33, No. 5 (May 1976), 548–55.

RASKOB, HEDWIG, "Logotherapy and Religion." *The International Forum for Logotherapy,* Vol. 1, No. 3 (Spring 1980), 8–12.

RELINGER, HELMUT, PHILIP H. BORNSTEIN, and DAN M. MUNGAS, "Treatment of Insomnia by Paradoxical Intention: A Time-Series Analysis." *Behavior Therapy,* Vol. 9 (1978), 955–59.

RICHMOND, BERT O., ROBERT L. MASON and VIRGINIA SMITH, "Existential Frustration and Anomie." *Journal of Women's Deans and Counselors* (Spring 1969).

ROBERTS, HELEN C., "Logotherapy's Contribution to Youth." *The International Forum for Logotherapy,* Vol. 1, No. 3 (Spring 1980), 19–21.

ROSE, HERBERT H., "Viktor Frankl on Conscience and God." *The Jewish Spectator* (Fall 1976), 49–50.

ROWLAND, STANLEY J., JR., "Viktor Frankl and the Will to Meaning." *Christian Century,* LXXIX (June 6, 1962), 722–24.

RUCKER, W. RAY, "Frankl's Contributions to the Graduate Program at the USIU." *The International Forum for Logotherapy,* Vol. 1, No. 3 (Spring 1980), 12.

RUGGIERO, VINCENT R., "Concentration Camps Were His Laboratory." *The Sign,* XLVII (Dec. 1967), 13–15.

SAHAKIAN, WILLIAM S., and BARBARA JACQUELYN SAHAKIAN, "Logotherapy As a Personality Theory." *The Israel Annals of Psychiatry and Related Disciplines,* X (1972), 230–44.

SARGENT, GEORGE ANDREW, "Job Satisfaction. Job Involvement and Purpose in Life: A Study of Work and Frankl's Will to Meaning." Thesis presented to the faculty of the United States International University in partial fulfillment of the requirements for the degree Master of Arts, 1971.

————, "Motivation and Meaning: Frankl's Logotherapy in the Work Situation." Dissertation, United States International University, San Diego, 1973.

SCHACHTER, STANLEY J., "Bettelheim and Frankl: Contradicting Views of the Holocaust." *Reconstructionist,* XXVI, No. 20 (Feb. 10, 1961), 6–11.

SHEA, JOHN J., "On the Place of Religion in the Thought of Viktor Frankl." *Journal of Psychology and Theology,* III, No. 3 (Summer 1975), 179–86.

SIMMS, GEORGE R., "Logotherapy in Medical Practice." *The International Forum for Logotherapy,* Vol. 2, No. 2 (Summer-Fall 1979), 12–14.

SOLYOM, L., J. GARZA-PEREZ, B. L. LEDWIDGE and C. SOLYOM, "Paradoxical Intention in the Treatment of Obsessive Thoughts: A Pilot Study." *Comprehensive Psychiatry*, Vol. 13, No. 3 (May 1972), 291–97.

STROPKO, ANDREW JOHN, "Logoanalysis and Guided Imagery as Group Treatments for Existential Vacuum." Dissertation, Texas Tech University, 1975.

TURNER, R. H., "Comment on Dr. Frankl's Paper." *Journal of Existential Psychiatry*, I (1960), 21–23.

TURNER, RALPH M., and L. MICHAEL ASCHER, "Controlled Comparison of Progressive Relaxation, Stimulus Control, and Paradoxical Intention Therapies for Insomnia." *Journal of Consulting and Clinical Psychology*, Vol. 47, No. 3 (1979), 500–08.

VanKAAM, ADRIAN, "Foundation Formation and the Will to Meaning." *The International Forum for Logotherapy*, Vol. 1, No. 3 (Spring 1980), 57–59.

VICTOR, RALPH G., and CAROLYN M. KRUG, "Paradoxical Intention in the Treatment of Compulsive Gambling." *American Journal of Psychotherapy*, XXI, No. 4 (Oct. 1967), 808–14.

"Viktor Frankl." *The Colby Alumnus*, LI (Spring 1962), 5.

WAUGH, ROBERT J. L., "Paradoxical Intention." *American Journal of Psychiatry*, Vol. 123, No. 10 (Apr. 1967), 1305–06.

WEISS, M. DAVID, "Frankl's Approach to the Mentally Ill." *Association of Mental Hospital Chaplains' Newsletter* (Fall 1962), 39–42.

WEISSKOPF-JOELSON, EDITH, "Some Comments on a Viennese School of Psychiatry." *Journal of Abnormal and Social Psychology*, LI (1955), 701–03.

———, "Logotherapy and Existential Analysis." *Acta Psychotherapeutica*, VI (1958), 193–204.

———, "Paranoia and the Will-to-Meaning." *Existential Psychiatry*, I (1966), 316–20.

———, "Some Suggestions Concerning the Concept of Awareness." *Psychotherapy: Theory, Research and Practice*, VIII (1971), 2–7.

———, "Logotherapy: Science or Faith?" *Psychotherapy: Theory, Research and Practice*, XII (1975), 238–40.

———, "The Place of Logotherapy in the World Today." *The International Forum for Logotherapy*, Vol. 1, No. 3 (Spring 1980), 3–7.

WILSON, ROBERT A., "Logotherapy: An Educational Approach for the Classroom Teacher." Laurence University, 1979.

WIRTH, ARTHUR G., "Logotherapy and Education in a Post-Petroleum Society." *The International Forum for Logotherapy*, Vol. 1, No. 3 (Spring 1980), 29–32.

YEATES, J. W., "The Educational Implications of the Logotherapy of Viktor E. Frankl." Doctoral dissertation, University of Mississippi, 1968.

4. FILMS, RECORDS, AND TAPES

FRANKL, VIKTOR E., "Logotherapy," a film produced by the Department of Psychiatry, Neurology, and Behavioral Sciences, University of Oklahoma Medical School.

————, "Frankl and the Search for Meaning," a film produced by Psychological Films, 110 North Wheeler Street, Orange, CA 92669.

————, "Some Clinical Aspects of Logotherapy. Paper read before the Anderson County Medical Society in South Carolina," "Man in Search of Meaning. Address given to the Annual Meeting of the Anderson County Mental Health Association in South Carolina," and "Man's Search for Ultimate Meaning. Lecture given at the Peachtree Road Methodist Church in Atlanta, Georgia," videotapes cleared for television upon request from WGTV, the University of Georgia, Athens, GA 30601.

————, "Meaning and Purpose in Human Experience," a videotape produced by Rockland Community College. Rental or purchase through the Director of Library Services, 145 College Road, Suffern, NY 10901.

————, "Education and the Search for Meaning. An Interview by Professor William Blair Gould of Bradley University," a videotape produced by Bradley University Television. Available by request from Bradley University, Peoria, IL 61606 ($25 handling charges for usage).

————, "Youth in Search for Meaning. The Third Paul Dana Bartlett Memorial Lecture," a videotape produced by KNBU and cleared for television upon request from President James Edward Doty, Baker University, Baldwin City, KA 66006.

——, "Clinical Aspects of Logotherapy," a videotaped lecture. Replay available by arrangement with Medical Illustration Services, Veterans Administration Hospital, 3801 Miranda Avenue, Palo Alto, CA 94304.

——, "Logotherapy," a videotaped lecture. Available for rental or purchase from Educational Television, University of California School of Medicine, Department of Psychiatry, Langley Porter Neuropsychiatric Institute, 3rd Avenue and Parnassus Avenue, San Francisco, CA 94112.

——, "Logotherapy Workshop," a videotaped lecture. Available for rental or purchase from Middle Tennessee State University, Learning Resource Center, Murfreesboro, TN 37130.

——, "The Rehumanization of Psychotherapy. A Workshop Sponsored by the Division of Psychotherapy of the American Psychological Association," a videotape. Address inquiries to Division of Psychotherapy, American Psychological Association, 1200 Seventeenth Street, N.W., Washington, DC 20036.

——, "Youth in Search of Meaning," a videotape produced by the Youth Corps and Metro Cable Television. Contact: Youth Corps, 56 Bond Street, Toronto, Ontario M5B 1X2, Canada. Rental fee $10.00.

——, "Man in Search of Meaning," a film interview with Jim Corey of CFTO Television in Toronto. Contact: Youth Corps, 56 Bond Street, Toronto, Ontario M5B 1X2, Canada.

——, "Human Freedom and Meaning in Life" and "Self-Transcendence—Therapeutic Agent in Sexual Neurosis," videotapes. Copies of the tapes can be ordered for a service fee. Address inquiries to the Manager, Learning Resource Distribution Center, United States International University, San Diego, CA 92131.

——, Two 5-hour lectures, part of the course *Human Behavior 616*, "Man in Search of Meaning," during the winter quarter, 1976. Copies of the videotapes can be ordered for a service fee. Address inquiries to the Manager, Learning Resource Distribution Center, United States International University, San Diego, CA 92131.

——, A videotaped convocation. Address inquiries to President Stephen Walsh, St. Edward's University, Austin, TX 78704.

————, A videotaped lecture given at Monash University, Melbourne, Australia, on March 6, 1976. Inquiries should be addressed to Royal Australian College of General Practitioners, Family Medicine Programme, Audio Visual Department, 70 Jolimont Street, Jolimont 3002, Melbourne, Australia.

————, "The Unheard Cry for Meaning," a videotape produced by the Youth Corps and Metropolitan Separate School Board of Toronto. Contact: Youth Corps, 56 Bond Street, Toronto, Ontario M5B 1X2, Canada. Rental fee $10.00.

————, Interview with Dr. Viktor E. Frankl by Dr. Paul W. Ngui, President, Singapore Association for Mental Health; 16 mm. film. Inquiries should be addressed to Controller, Central Production Unit, Television Singapore, Singapore, 10.

————, "Three Lectures on Logotherapy," given at the Brandeis Institute, Brandeis, CA 93064. Long-playing records.

————, "Man in Search of Meaning: Two Dialogues," "Self-Transcendence: The Motivational Theory of Logotherapy," "What Is Meant by Meaning?" and "Logotherapy and Existentialism," audiotapes produced by Jeffrey Norton Publishers, Inc., 145 East 49th Street, New York, NY 10017.

————, "The Student's Search for Meaning," an audiotape produced by WGTV, the University of Georgia, Athens, GA 30601.

————, "The Existential Vacuum" ("Existential Frustration As a Challenge to Psychiatry," "Logotherapy As a Concept of Man," "Logotherapy As a Philosophy of Life"), tapes produced by Argus Communications, 7440 Natchez Avenue, Niles, IL 60648. $18.00.

————, "The Existential Vacuum: A Challenge to Psychiatry. Address given at The Unitarian Church, San Francisco, California, October 13, 1969," a tape produced by Big Sur Recordings, 2015 Bridgeway, Sausalito, CA 94965.

————, "Meaninglessness: Today's Dilemma," an audiotape produced by Creative Resources, 4800 West Waco Drive, Waco, TX 76703.

————, "Logotherapy Workshop," an audiotape produced by Middle Tennessee State University, Learning Resource Center, Murfreesboro, Tennessee 37130.

————, "Man's Search for Meaning. An Introduction to Logotherapy." Recording for the Blind, Inc., 215 East 58th Street, New York, NY 10022.

————, "Youth in Search of Meaning." Word Cassette Library (WCL 0205), 4800 West Waco Drive, Waco, TX 76703 ($5.95).

————, Lecture given at Monash University, Melbourne, Australia, on March 6, 1976. An audiocassette available from Spectrum Publications, 127 Burnley Street, Richmond, Victoria 3121, Australia.

————, "Theory and Therapy of Neurosis: A Series of Lectures Delivered at the United States International University in San Diego, California." Eight 90-minute cassettes produced by Creative Resources, 4800 West Waco Drive, Waco, TX 76703 ($79.95).

————, "Man in Search of Meaning: A Series of Lectures Delivered at the United States International University in San Diego, California." Fourteen 90-minute cassettes produced by Creative Resources, 4800 West Waco Drive, Waco, TX 76703 ($139.95).

————, "The Neurotization of Humanity and the Re-Humanization of Psychotherapy," two cassettes. Argus Communications, 7440 Natchez Avenue, Niles, IL 60648 ($14.00).

————, "Youth in Search of Meaning," an audiotape produced by the Youth Corps, 56 Bond Street, Toronto, Ontario M5B 1X2, Canada. Available on reel-to-reel or cassette. $7.50.

————, "The Unheard Cry for Meaning," an audiocassette produced by the Youth Corps, 56 Bond Street, Toronto, Ontario M5B 1X2, Canada. $6.50.

————, "Therapy Through Meaning," Psychotherapy Tape Library (T 656), Psychotherapy and Social Science Review, 111 Eighth Ave., New York, NY 10011 ($15.00).

————, "The Defiant Power of the Human Spirit: A Message of Meaning in a Chaotic World." Address at the Berkeley Community Theater, November 2, 1979. A 90-minute cassette tape, available at the Institute of Logotherapy, One Lawson Road, Berkeley, CA 94707 ($6.00).

————, and HUSTON SMITH, "Value Dimensions in Teaching," a color television film produced by Hollywood Animators, Inc., for the California Junior College Association. Rental or purchase through Dr. Rex Wignall, Director, Chaffey College, Alta Loma, CA 91701.

————, ROBIN W. GOODENOUGH, IVER HAND, OLIVER A. PHILLIPS and EDITH WEISSKOPF-JOELSON, "Logotherapy: Theory and Practice. A Symposium Sponsored by the

Division of Psychotherapy of the American Psychological Association," an audiotape. Address inquiries to Division of Psychotherapy, American Psychological Association, 1200 Seventeenth Street, N.W., Washington, DC 20036.

GALE, RAYMOND F., JOSEPH FABRY, MARY ANN FINCH and ROBERT C. LESLIE, "A Conversation with Viktor E. Frankl on Occasion of the Inauguration of the 'Frankl Library and Memorabilia' at the Graduate Theological Union on February 12, 1977," a videotape. Copies may be obtained from Professor Robert C. Leslie, 1798 Scenic Avenue, Berkeley, CA 94709.

HALE, DR. WILLIAM H., "An Interview with Viktor E. Frankl. With an Introduction by Dr. Edith Weisskopf-Joelson, Professor of Psychology at the University of Georgia," a videotape cleared for television upon request from WGTV, the University of Georgia, Athens, GA 30601.

————, "The Humanistic Revolution: Pioneers in Perspective," interviews with leading humanistic psychologists: Abraham Maslow, Garner Murphy, Carl Rogers, Rollo May, Paul Tillich, Frederick Perls, Viktor Frankl and Alan Watts. Psychological Films, 1215 East Chapman Ave., Orange, CA 92666. Sale $250; rental $20.

MURRAY, DR. EDWARD L., and DR. ROLF VON ECKARTS-BERG, A Discussion with Dr. Viktor E. Frankl on "Logotherapy: Theory and Applied" conducted by two members of the Duquesne University Graduate School of Psychology, filmed July 25, 1972. Available for rental, fee $15. Mail request to Chairman, Department of Psychology, Duquesne University, Pittsburgh, PA 15219.

5. BRAILLE EDITIONS

FABRY, JOSEPH B., *The Pursuit of Meaning: Logotherapy Applied to Life.*

FRANKL, VIKTOR E., *Man's Search for Meaning: An Introduction to Logotherapy.*

———, *The Unheard Cry for Meaning: Psychotherapy and Humanism.*

Braille editions of the above three books are available on loan at no cost from Woodside Terrace Kiwanis Braille Project, 850 Longview Road, Hillsborough, CA 94010.

About the Author

VIKTOR E. FRANKL IS PROFESSOR OF NEUROLOGY and PSYCHIATRY at the University of Vienna Medical School and Distinguished Professor of Logotherapy at the U.S. International University. He is the founder of what has come to be called the Third Viennese School of Psychotherapy (after Freud's psychoanalysis and Adler's individual psychology)—the school of logotherapy.

Born in 1905, Dr. Frankl received the degrees of Doctor of Medicine and Doctor of Philosophy from the University of Vienna. During World War II he spent three years at Auschwitz, Dachau and other concentration camps.

Dr. Frankl first published in 1924 in the INTERNATIONAL JOURNAL OF PSYCHOANALYSIS and has since published twenty-seven books, which have been translated into nineteen languages, including Japanese and Chinese. He has been a visiting professor at Harvard, Duquesne and Southern Methodist Universities. Honorary Degrees have been conferred upon him by Loyola University in Chicago, Edgecliff College, Rockford College and Mount Mary College, as well as by universities in Brazil, Venezuela, and South Africa. He has been a guest lecturer at universities throughout the world and has made fifty-two lecture tours throughout the United States alone. He is President of the Austrian Medical Society of Psychotherapy and Honorary Member of the Austrian Academy of Sciences.